COMMUNITY
HERITAGE
LEGACY

IN PURSUIT OF PROGRESS
SELECTED SPEECHES, PAPERS, ESSAYS

COMMUNITY
HERITAGE
LEGACY

IN PURSUIT OF PROGRESS
SELECTED SPEECHES, PAPERS, ESSAYS

MELVIN S. ZARET

PRINTSTAR
BOOKS

Edited by Gail Naron Chalew
Cover and text design by Georgene Schreiner

2010 09 08 07 06   5   4   3   2   1

Printed in the United States of America

First printing 2006

ISBN-10: 0-9702518-6-6
ISBN-13: 978-0-9702518-6-2

Published by Printstar Publishing, LLC.
633 W. Wisconsin Ave., Suite 1008, Milwaukee, Wisconsin
(414) 640-9377
www.ppub.com

The Meaning of Life

What an extraordinary situation is that of us mortals! Each of us is here for a brief sojourn; for what purpose he knows not, though he sometimes thinks he feels it. But from the point of view of daily life, without going deeper, we exist for our fellow-men—in the first place for those on whose smiles and welfare all our happiness depends, and next for all those unknown to us personally with whose destinies we are bound up by the tie of sympathy. A hundred times every day I remind myself that my inner and outer life depend on the labors of other men, living and dead, and that I must exert myself in order to give in the same measure as I have received and am still receiving.

From *The World As I See It*

by Albert Einstein

The Wisdom Library, a Division of the Philosophical Library—1949

Table of Contents

Foreword

The publication before you incarnates an important voice that deserves to be heard—the voice of Mel Zaret. Mel Zaret's is an epic life; it reflects and tracks the remarkable history of the past 70 years. This era represents the most extraordinary stretch of the journey of the Jewish people through history toward the perfection of the world.

Mel Zaret was a typical Jewish young man striving to Americanize—as was the whole American Jewish community. He took Jewish idealism and love of humanity and translated it into his work as an executive of a small agency working with troubled boys in Chicago. (This same Jewish idealism was harnessed in thousands of cases to serve humanity and to improve the world.) Then Mel went into the army in World War II carrying on the responsibilities of Jewish patriotism to this blessed country. In the Great War, he encountered the Holocaust. This turned him to the path of healing the Jewish people and rebuilding as his contribution to tikkun olam. He determined to stay in Milwaukee—where his work, his passion, his devotion, and his intelligence could make a difference. He entered the world of federation and sought to develop the model Jewish community—a community that would rebuild Jewish life, be a good neighbor and be a good citizen of the general society while reaching out to Jewish people all over the world with help and affection to sustain them and confirm them on their Jewish path.

Over the years Mel built the Milwaukee Jewish Federation as a training ground for Jewish professionals who went all over the Jewish world and became leaders and servants of the Jewish people in their own right. He built a community that reached out to all its members without discrimination and without denying the validity and value of every denomination and need. He built a community that was a source of help and life for Jewry locally, nationally and internationally.

Mel is a person of discretion and dedication, and he is always selfless enough to do the job without injecting his own agendas. Mel always looked for ways to help and connect and did not seek the honors to be upfront but rather to get the job done and to enable the best in others. Over the years therefore he was trusted and given tasks to do by JDC, CJF, HIAS, and JAFI. He advised Jewish communities in Brazil and Belgium and Europe and Israel. He offered them help and made connections. In many cases those communities sent people to train in Milwaukee in order to improve their skills and their ability to work at home. Thus this quiet but skilled leader continued to be a source of blessing for his profession, for his community, for the world of federations, and for Jewish communities.

Mel always looked for the opportunity to help new constructive forces. My personal account of my relationship with him began when I came to Milwaukee in the early days of CLAL. He recognized the need. He personally brought CLAL in to set up classes in Milwaukee. He personally attended Shabbatonim and participated in the spirit and joy as well as the learning and the practice of Judaism. I will never forget that he met and fell in love with Eva, herself a survivor, whose life had been deeply shaped by her experience in the Holocaust. I was privileged to organize a ceremony of celebration for them. The collective joy was a reaffirmation of life and of love; it expressed the eternal hope and the unbroken zest for life of Mel and Eva as individuals and of the Jewish people as a people.

In this publication a series of papers, talks, and reports are being brought together. Study them and you will learn the wisdom of the Jewish religion that teaches that every day and in everyday acts of life and in the activities of community building lies the secret of redemption. This volume proves—as does Mel Zaret's life—that as long as Jews care, as long as people of skill and commitment and Jewish spirit are prepared to step up and take responsibility for their time, their place, and their community, the promise of the eternal life of the Jewish people will be fulfilled.

— *Rabbi Irving Greenberg*
  President, Jewish Life Network/Steinhardt Foundation

Introduction

This volume contains speeches given, essays, and papers written over a period of more than fifty years on issues pertaining to Jewish communities and the Jewish world. Many of the speeches were presentations at General Assemblies of the Council of Jewish Federations (now the United Jewish Communities), the largest annual gathering of volunteer and professional Jewish community leaders in North America. Also included are speeches given at National Conferences of Jewish Communal Service; a few were presentations in Milwaukee where I served for twenty-nine years, until 1984, as the Jewish Federation executive, and where I've lived and worked for more than sixty years. Several of the essays were prepared for publication by journals for professionals and volunteers in Jewish communal service. Every effort has been made to diminish repetition, except when required to bridge the flow of thought.

Since each was at the invitation of a sponsoring body already aware of my thoughts, many reflect the progressive reasoning and ideas of the era on these subjects—both mine and of my professional and voluntary colleagues. Where a principle is enunciated it is, however, meant to be long lasting, modified, of course, by the lessons of time.

In preparing these papers, I've had to transpose some from speech to essay form. Though speeches or papers were for varying groups over a long period, they're interconnected, for they all focus on the Jewish people and Jewish community life in America and in other countries where I've had opportunities to work.

The Jews are an ancient people like no other, retaining continuity through thousands of years, even without a land of their own. Dispersed throughout the world, they constitute a small minority, a trickle in the flood of humanity, with great diversity and yet a distinctive unity.

The ideas of the Jewish federation and the voluntary community are the unique American Jewish contribution to the Jewish world. A federation is a special kind of association based on a mutual past and civic friendship that is designed to promote noble actions, to improve life, and to ensure survival as a people. Each federation is a vehicle through which Jewish people in a community unite, dealing with local matters of concern and then with other communities everywhere and with Israel as one. This spirit of identity and oneness by people dispersed for so long is a miracle distinct only to the Jews, a wondrous people with the depth and width of the skies of Jerusalem on one's first visit.

The wonder of the Jews stirs interest and study at centers for Jewish studies, found now even in countries from which they were expelled and in which they were persecuted and suppressed, such as in the former Soviet Union, in Germany, in Spain, and in Romania; sometimes these centers have been initiated by non-Jews. Centers for Jewish studies exist even in China, in major universities developed by the Chinese with Chinese professors and primarily Chinese students.

These papers may seem like they belong to the past and they do. But the past has not really passed—it lives on in the present. Respected writers and philosophers have written of the past. Marcel Proust said, "The past is not fugitive, it remains present." Spinoza wrote, "If you want the present to be different from the past—study the past." And Kierkegaard said, "Life must be lived forward but can only be understood backward."

Of course the past is irretrievable. It should, however, be known and understood so its errors are not repeated and so that we avoid having the future become a sad, remorseful, bitter look backward. We must learn from the past. Jonathan Swift wrote that, "Invention is the talent of youth, but judgment is the talent of experience and age."

Though I think of myself as humanist in orientation with special concern for the Jewish world, I've been particularly attached to the Milwaukee Jewish community. I met and worked there with a collective leadership as fine as that found anywhere in the world. And I've had the good fortune to work with good, outstanding professionals who came from elsewhere and joined me in Milwaukee early in their careers: more of them went on to be executives in major national and international agencies than from any community of Milwaukee's size. The same applies to voluntary leaders with whom I've worked and who have been a major influence on the continental and world Jewish scene.

Throughout my work life I've been privileged to work with and observe so many Jewish communities in the United States, Canada, Europe, South America, and Israel. These experiences underscored my feeling that leadership in Milwaukee was as fine as found anywhere and the conviction that Milwaukee could be a model for others to emulate. I still believe it can be.

I acknowledge with deep-felt appreciation the role of the Milwaukee Jewish Federation and especially its Jewish Community Foundation for encouraging me to create this volume. I'm especially grateful for the supportive role of the Foundation's executive, Bert Bilsky, with whom I had the privilege of working for a brief time, enough to convince me that he would be a force in helping Milwaukee travel a path toward securing itself as a precious community.

I acknowledge with thanks and respect the role of the Foundation's chairman, Mark Brickman, who has served as campaign chairman and federation president and who has never faltered in his devotion to Jewish community life and to the welfare and advancement of humankind. Our long-time treasured friendship is founded in the furnace of mutual concerns.

I was fortunate enough to have Gail Naron Chalew edit this work with skill that exceeded even the high opinions of those who brought her to my attention. She helped shape this work. It would be difficult to overstate my respect and thanks for her help.

PART I:
Fundamentals of Community Organization

FINANCING OF THE JEWISH COMMUNITY: PRESENT AND FUTURE

Keynote address at Western Canada Community Assembly in Calgary, Alberta

October 1982

GOALS

In the middle of 1979, during a meeting of the Council of Jewish Federations, an ambitious goal of raising $1 billion by 1984 was set. This goal represented a doubling of the approximately $500 million being raised at that time. To reach it, there would need to be an increase close to 15 percent in each of the next five years.

Are we on the way to realizing this ambitious goal? In 1980, U.S. Jewry raised $538 million; in 1981, $578 million; and in 1982, we will raise approximately $600 million. If we project this same rate of increase for the next two years—7% as opposed to the goal of 15%—we will raise about $690 million, far short of the hoped-for $1 billion, in 1984. This amount approximates what we raised in 1974, stimulated then by the Yom Kippur War. Yet, during the intervening decade, the needs have grown, but so has the giving capacity of the Jewish community.

The $1 billion dollar fundraising goal may have been established blithely, but those who thought boldly saw it as a firmly fixed, achievable target.

A self-study by the United Israel Appeal of Canada in 1981 established similar targets. That study, a blueprint for the future, projected a goal for the year 1986 of $100 million compared with the 1981 fundraising achievement of $55 million. However, because of a projected inflation rate of 12.6%, the $100 million goal would just enable the Canadian community to stay even. The study also noted that campaigns had in general been stagnant since the Yom Kippur War or, at best, had merely overcome the inflation factor. It stressed the views of partner and beneficiary agencies that the funds raised did not meet even the basic needs of the Canadian Jewish community. The report concluded by providing specific year-by year fundraising targets, taking into account increases in Jewish wealth as well as inflation.

This is a wise study. I was impressed with its emphasis on the inseparability of domestic Jewish communal needs from those of the people of Israel and the intertwining of the fortunes of each Canadian Jewish community with the other.

On the local level, I look at the community in which I live. In 1980, Milwaukee raised about $6,400,000. At the time, looking ahead we projected a need for far more than twice that amount just to cope with inflation and some relatively well-known additional needs. Achieving such goals requires serious work preceded by careful thought.

Communities, like people, are models, one for the other. Thus, the Jewish communities in the United States and Canada are inseparable, just as each is linked with Israel and with all Jewish communities on all continents—tied together by a common past and common bond.

PROBLEMS IN THE AMERICAN ECONOMY

Economic factors do of course affect fundraising. Setbacks in the economy, which reduce income and wealth, can be costly. We now face double-digit inflation. It was sneaking up on us like a thief, but now it moves straight at us like an enemy, eroding our resources. Even as we raise more money, we are able to do less. In response, our Jewish communities have monitored costs carefully, reducing overhead and other costs where possible, dropping unnecessary services, and merging agencies. Some communities have reduced hours of operation of Jewish community centers and even, in some instances, the dollar limits of the amount of rents subsidized for Soviet refugees coming into our communities. Our collective conscience pains us.

GOVERNMENTAL FUNDS

The Jewish community has only in recent years begun to develop an expertise in the use of public dollars. We always feared that our programs could be looked upon negatively if we used public money. Thus, we took care of our own, to a greater degree than any other group. It is as though we were pursuing a contract made in 1654 with Peter Stuyvesant when we agreed to take care of our own in exchange for permission for Jews to settle in this newly developing continent.

In recent years, we had begun to behave as full partners in American society. When the Soviet Union set its doors slightly ajar and Jews began to leave as refugees, we negotiated a block grant with the U.S. government to help us in the resettlement of Russian refugees. The grant, which was obtained by the Council of Jewish Federations, was in the many millions of dollars, approximately $1,000 for each refugee. This was a great blessing for these Soviet American Jews and for Jewish communities worldwide.

Jewish hospitals and homes for the aged have also received hundreds of millions of dollars in government funding. Government grants have flowed to family agencies, vocational services, and JCCs, easing the burdens carried by the Jewish community. Jewish educational organizations, particularly day schools, have received government aid to meet food costs under certain circumstances.

TAX CUTS

Now an economic problem is posed by tax cuts with their terribly negative consequences for human services. Liberal thinking has been set aside; it seems that candidates for office today automatically gain votes by advocating a reduction in taxes. Funding for government social welfare programs has been cut back and eligibility requirements tightened, producing suffering in their wake. In New York, the federation reports that 300,000 Jews live at or below the poverty level. Philadelphia has lost a $2 million public service employment program. The Jewish Vocational Service in Milwaukee, one of the largest such agencies in any community in the world, has lost millions of dollars previously available to it through a variety of governmental grants. Our

Jewish communities are hard put to compete for dollars with other segments of the population.

As good citizens, we hardly favor waste in government. The headlines that greet us about millions in waste here and there are not pleasing. But they please us even less when they represent false accusations. The field of public welfare has become a handy target and often a scapegoat. That is something we, as a people, know something about. Poor people, those who suffer the most by these cuts, have little power.

OTHER REVENUE SOURCES

Although corporate giving increased in 1981 by 11%, it hardly fills the gap. This meager increase comes despite recent changes in the tax code that raise tax deductibility for corporate giving from 5% to 10% of profits. It is wrong to assume, however, that this change in the tax law will have a major impact on private philanthropy. In most cities, corporate giving amounts to only 1% of profits. In Minneapolis, there is a club for corporations that give away 5% of their profits, but it has only 45 member corporations. One of the leaders of the 5% club, Kenneth Dayton of the Dayton-Hudson Corporation, acknowledged, "Compared with potential corporate giving, the record is dismal."

The United Way is another source of funds for agency services. At the high point of funding in 1975 it funded 30% of the budgets of Jewish local agencies. As agency budgets grew, it provided less proportionately—27% in 1978—and the percentage has been going down ever since. The importance of the United Way as a funding resource differs from city to city: 25.9% of money budgeted by the Buffalo Jewish Federation comes from the United Way, in contrast to 12.4% of money budgeted in Cleveland and only 9.3% in Chicago.

There is no clear-cut method of allocation for United Way funds in the Jewish community nor is there a uniform system in which Jewish communities obtain such funds. There will probably need to be one. When federations develop an overall community budget to meet the needs of the entire Jewish community, not just a need of an individual agency or group, it is probable that more money will be forthcoming. For the present, federations operate on a deficit financing basis with agencies supported by the United Way, such as community centers and Jewish Family Services, but continue to shoulder the primary financial responsibility.

Another source of revenue is provided by fees that people pay for services. We are less and less an immigrant and poor population requiring settlement houses and financial aid. The people who use our agencies are better able to pay for services than in earlier years and often feel slighted when they are not asked to pay them, though we consider it right that we aid people who truly need services for which they cannot pay.

PRIVATE FOUNDATIONS

Another type of funding, private foundation grants, has not yet become a major source of funds for federations. It has been flat in recent years. But foundations are growing quickly and can be looked to in the near future as a major source of funds. We must, at the same time, take into account that Jewish people who have gained in wealth and who establish these foundations, once discriminated against by most civic organizations, are now welcomed on the boards of directors of art, music, cultural organizations and universities. One reason Jewish donors are welcomed is the hope and expectation that these institutions will be the recipients of grants from such sources. Nevertheless, the Jewish community may expect in the future that private foundations will be a substantial source of funds, but the time is not here now.

JEWISH COMMUNITY ENDOWMENT FUNDS

One of the largest sources of money for our federations in years to come will be our own endowment funds. Endowment funds within federations are providing support for programs that would otherwise not exist, including projects developed on a trial basis and funds to meet emergency needs.

At the end of 1981, all of our communities collectively held approximately $600 million in their endowment funds. In the several years before 1980, federations had made grants of $188 million from their endowments. A business cannot succeed if it is under-capitalized; working capital is needed to make growth possible. Philanthropy has become big business and Jewish philanthropy is very precious. We need to secure it as we secure ourselves and our children. The endowment programs or Jewish Community Foundation, however they are called, is a primary source for that security in the future.

My community, like so many others, developed its endowment—the Jewish Community Foundation—only recently. In 1979, we held about $2 million dollars in reserve, and a year later, that figure had grown to $3,224,000. In the 2.5 years since, the endowment has grown to exceed $8 million in various funds, nearly $5 million of it in philanthropic funds in which the donor retains the privilege of advising on expenditures.

Grants from these funds have gone to fund Jewish education, transportation for the elderly, programs focusing on Israel, and such specialized needs as education for women in social services. In the last few years, grants have been made to approximately 100 different organizations and the amount of money expended has been growing. Like any other self-respecting endowment program, we hold institutes to educate lawyers, accountants, and estate planners, and provide seminars for women who seek education in financial management.

Sometimes the question is posed as to why the federation is so involved with those funds in which donors retain advisory rights. The answer is that Jewish life is the greatest beneficiary of these funds. The donor receives guidance and expert help, which they appreciate. The director of the foundation in my own city is an attorney, but he was also a professional social worker and executive of an agency. His legal and social welfare background qualifies him to help guide the endowment fund. Once properly created and developed, such programs mean ongoing income to the federation.

Endowment programs are the wave of the future. I foresee foundations being the largest single source of capital funding for federations. Endowment programs may well become a basic source of money to reduce the massive Jewish Agency debt; if that debt did not exist, then the $100 million currently paid by the Jewish Agency in interest would be available for constructive purposes in the Galilee or in the Negev, in settlements for newcomers, for Aliyah, and for the strengthening of Israel.

The declining proportion of funds from the United Way, the modest amount of money available from major corporations, the lack of development of private foundations as a major source of money, and the relatively recent development of endowment programs within our own federations mean that, at this moment, we need to look primarily to individuals for funds. The amount from individuals approximates 84% of all money given to philanthropy.

Fortunately, individual philanthropy is growing in the United States: individuals gave $53.6 billion dollars to philanthropy in 1981, an increase of 12.3% over the previous year.

THE GIVING POPULATION

Two academicians who studied philanthropy in the Boston Jewish community reported their findings in a paper entitled "Will the Well Run Dry? The Future of Jewish Giving in America." They found a correlation between giving and Jewish involvement. Those who are active in Jewish life in one way or another—either by attending synagogue services, participating in Jewish cultural activities, keeping Kosher homes, having Mezzuahs on their doors, lighting Sabbath candles, reading magazines of Jewish interest, or involving themselves in the work of Jewish agencies, or the federation—give more than those who are not actively involved. The more Jewish one's behavior is, however it is measured, the more likely one is to give. Clearly, the Jewish enterprise depends upon the Jewishness of the Jews.

In this connection, Canadian Jewry has an advantage over American Jewry. Jews in the United States had generations earlier, being fearful of prejudice, emphasized integration into the general American scene at the expense of their Jewishness. We worked to erase the special qualities that made us different and saw being accepted by others as key to our acceptance of ourselves. It is only in more recent years that we have learned to reaffirm a special Jewish spirit and Jewish distinctiveness and to nourish Jewish values.

In contrast, because the exclusionary immigration laws of the United States prevented people from entering from the 1920s onward, Canada received proportionately more immigrants and more Holocaust survivors during that time. Canadian Jewry is a generation closer to the Old World than are American Jews. Concentrated into specific geographic areas, Canadian

Jews are generally more Jewish than American Jews. They speak more Yiddish, provide their children with more intensive Jewish education, make higher per capita contributions, have lower rates of intermarriage, and visit Israel more frequently.

The United States and Canada also have different ideas about cultural diversity. The United States always prided itself on being a melting pot—on the assimilation of people into one identity of Americanism. It called upon immigrants to give up their previous identities in exchange for new American ones. In contrast, Canada always encouraged ethnic groups to retain their ancestral identity and heritage. In the ethnic mosaic that is Canada, Canadian Jews were encouraged to keep their distinctive Jewish identity.

Philanthropy is basic to our religious beliefs. After all, even the most religious of Jews specify that the most important thing in life, in addition to belief in God and prayer, is giving—tzedakah. The concept of tzedakah has helped bind us together and preserve us as a people for these thousands of years as we came to understand the admonition from the *Ethics of the Fathers:* "Honor not a man for his possessions, and honor him for the right use he makes of them."

A 1981 study done by the research director of the United Jewish Appeal found that 20% of all mega-millionaires, people with personal assets of over $50 million, are members of the Jewish community. He counted 460 Jewish people who hold major corporate positions or who are major shareholders in 202 top corporations in the Fortune 500 list. Yet, only 79 of these 460 people gave $10,000 or more.

Using criteria that admittedly may not be altogether scientific, that same research director estimated that there are 130 U.S. Jews with a capacity to contribute at the million-dollar level in annual campaigns. And the number of Jews of wealth is growing. Clearly, more money can be raised.

THE GOOD CAMPAIGN

How will we raise the money needed to meet Jewish community needs? Simple, by waging better campaigns. By and large, good campaigns take place in good communities. Where there is a community spirit and a sense of kinship among Jews, where all worthwhile activities are regarded as being the business of the whole community with federation involvement, where there is a warm and informed leadership, and where positions of status are occupied by people of stature, we raise more money. In the good community, people who are respected are sought out for leadership roles, and they serve willingly out of their regard for the community. In the good community, large numbers of people are involved in making decisions, and the decision makers represent a cross-section of the community. A good campaign community is one in which education of the worker and the giver takes place at home and in Israel on missions and in some instances, in alternative missions to Washington and New York. In a good community a good campaign includes study and evaluation of everything it does, and the next campaign is planned before the last one is concluded. By and large, a good campaign is planned long in advance and throughout the year—many months before the conduct of the campaign itself. In the good campaign, goals are based upon a real knowledge of community need, possessed not only by those who operate services but also by those who raise the money. The campaign goals become a reflection of need in dollar terms.

A good campaign is preceded by an extensive review of the capacity of people to give. Such "rating" by a peer group helps determine the request made of the donor and it's good business for it sends a message to givers that their peers care enough about each donor to exercise care in determining what campaign leaders and workers consider as a suitable gift.

CAMPAIGNS WITHIN A CAMPAIGN

There are sub-campaigns within a good campaign. The first sub-campaign takes place among the people who lead—the campaign chair, the federation president and executive, and other key leaders—those who are best known and most respected. The results should demonstrate the commitment of those who lead as examples and serve as a guide to people in the next sub-campaign grouping—divisional leaders and campaign workers. Then comes the next sub-campaign, board members of the federation and of agencies encompassed in the campaign—and then people associated with the national and international organizations identified with enriching Jewish life.

Unfortunately, only a minority of gifts in most community campaigns are a result of face-to-face discussions. The CJF Campaign Planning Advisory Committee found in a number of communities studied that only 8% of givers were being seen on a face-to-face basis. A key factor in determining the success of campaigns is the percentage of face-to-face solicitations, which communicate a message to the donor of the importance of his gift.

Another major determination of the quality of campaigns is the involvement of women. Women play a key role in the family, molding the opinion of the men who are the primary givers and educating children who are the future. In the good community, the women's division operates on a year-round basis. Thoroughgoing review has taught us that women generally study and learn more and transmit campaign fervor more effectively than do men. Women have grown in status in communities and more than ever share economic power. I confess to a personal bias for I live in a community where I have seen greatness flowing from the work of the year-round Women's Division in fundraising as well as in many other ways.

THE UNIFIED CAMPAIGN

In the tussle over the money required to meet human needs, those with a primary interest in Israel and less in the Diaspora often promulgate the idea of a separate campaign for Israel. How foolish that would be. The fact is that these separate campaigns have not worked well and probably never will. Think of the chaotic fundraising done by English Jewry, with a competition among organizations for funding.

The federation idea calls for unified fundraising—and it came into being to avoid the multiplicity of campaigns, which confused and annoyed community members. It is predicated upon an assumption that people in a community can develop a system through which a collective examination of need, and cooperation between agencies and institutions and the whole community can be mobilized to obtain money to meet those needs. That means that money requested is to fund human services that have been carefully examined and with demonstrated financial need. That's good business.

COORDINATING FUNDRAISING

Two years ago, at the General Assembly of the Council of Jewish Federations held in Detroit, in a major session on multiple appeals, a key leader of the Toronto Jewish community spoke of 160 testimonial dinners by various organizations in a single year—thoroughly creating impatience and disillusioning responsible leaders. To eliminate this multiplicity and confusion, key leaders and donors signed a pledge that they would not support any fundraising effort that had not been cleared and endorsed by the federation in advance. This of course, excepts bonds for Israel which it is understood, depends on major annual events to obtain essential investment income for Israel.

We do need to recognize that order and unity do not appeal to all people. A large cadre of professional campaigners who make a living from their work know that federation is an advanced idea that not all people grasp. Some can see only the particularistic thing with which they are specifically concerned. But if each person works only for his or her cause in competition with other people working for theirs, then what we have is the antithesis of community—disorganization—which misleads and bewilders givers.

In a campaign, we perform the mitzvah of tzedakah—the greatest of all mitzvot. We learn to live as one people, stressing our willingness, first as individuals, to share responsibilities with others, and then as communities to assume the proper share of responsibility for the survival and progress of an extraordinary people. We build unity, which builds Jewish life.

WHAT IS A CAMPAIGN?

This talk was given in a training session for campaign workers and became part of a guidebook for campaign leaders and workers.

1956

A CAMPAIGN IS ABOUT PEOPLE

A campaign is about hope. It is not only about refugees and suffering masses and the ransom of Jews but also about Jewish life, culture, art, and music. It is about jobs and food and homes. It is about the many thousands of families in countries around the world helped by the American Jewish Joint Distribution Committee. It is about the 80,000 Jews of Iran moving forward to the 20th century from the 9th century in which they now live. It is about the 110,000 Jews in Algeria whose families lived there from the time of the Romans and who were more indigenous to that land than the very Moslem majority that imperils their lives. It is about the 125,000 Algerian Jews who have moved to Paris, the 50,000 new inhabitants of Marseilles, and the thousands of new residents of Lyon and Toulouse and Bordeaux and Nice. It is about more than 70,000 of these Jews who will come to Israel in 1956, who will kiss the soil of freedom as they disembark from a plane or a ship.

A campaign is about the agencies of Jewish life that benefit the refugee, the emotionally disturbed, the sick, and the unemployed. It is about the Jewish schools that teach the young so that they will inherit the tradition of their ancestors and go forth to develop Jewish life.

We have shared in bringing 1,500,000 Jews to freedom in Israel. They have begun to live new lives, but even as we have helped these people, we recognize that we were doing only one-third of the job. Two-thirds of the cost of their absorption is paid for by the Israelis, most of whom are people of modest means. Any growth of unity among the surrounding nations of Iraq, Syria, Egypt, and Jordan, and the noose tightens around Israel. Israel lacks the resources to adequately defend itself while carrying two-thirds of the burden of absorption of immigrants, a responsibility that belongs to all of the Jews of the world, not just to Israel. It is our duty to share the burden, actually the opportunity, more equitably.

The anguish of the past is seared onto our souls and our minds—our memories of things past will never cease to be with us. Yet, out of our agony and despair comes a new determination. As doors open, the leaders and workers of communities must stand ready and waiting, bearing in mind the fact that the doors may close again, as they have done before. Opportunities to help must be grasped.

Am I my brother's keeper? The answer of workers and leaders to that question is a resounding "yes." But that answer is given meaning only by our deeds. The survival of the Jewish people is a woman descending from the gangplank of a ship and breathing in the new air of freedom in a free society; a child descending from a plane in Israel or New York or Boston or Rio de Janeiro; or a child less imperiled in Teheran or Tunis or Casablanca or Paris.

THE CAMPAIGN AND THE WORKER

Workers in a campaign are leaders. They are people who know that they are involved in a great endeavor out of which they take as much as they give. They are people dedicated to the survival of Judaism—concerned with their fellow human beings.

A campaign offers its workers the opportunity to reaffirm their idealism and fulfill their dream to strengthen Jewish life. For such workers, it is not enough to talk about Jewish principles and doctrines; they need to act on those principles—not to forsake the aged, to care for the sick, to ransom the captive, to minister to the poor, to educate the young, and to provide a haven for the homeless. Some Jews identify with these objectives out of religious motivations or out of a sense of peoplehood or just because they are kind and very good people. Why are workers involved? Out of a love for people, out of a fear about what the world could be if it were not for those who strive to make it better, and out of a desire to shape a better community.

Through our efforts, we enhance our own deep sense of conviction that each of us adds purpose to life, that we have meaning and value on this earth where we are placed for so short a time, and that we are of consequence to other people, who are dependent upon us and with whom our destinies are intertwined.

The success of the campaign is determined not by its structure but by who works and who leads and how they lead and how they work.

Good campaign workers ask not how little must I give, but how much can I give. They ask how they can best communicate this story to other people in the community. They know the giver and plan the solicitation approach carefully. They care enough to see every giver individually and never to discuss the needs in a telephone solicitation, not even a little bit. They are bold and courageous and dedicated and committed. They do more than just "cover the cards" for they know that the success of the campaign is not determined by how many people give, but by how much is given by each community member.

WHO IS THE GIVER?

Givers are people to whom we offer an opportunity—to enrich their own lives. A pledge card is not merely a piece of paper with a few simple words required by law. It is actually a unique big ticket to opportunity. It is a ticket that makes possible not only the sustenance of life for countless thousands but also is the ticket to freedom. For us, it is a ticket to our own self-respect and a sense of righteousness and dignity.

Pity the person who knows not how to give; respect and admire the ones who feel enriched by their own generosity when they give well. Much that is worthwhile in this world is made possible when people work together to achieve common objectives, to build a community. A good community makes for a better people, and each one who voluntarily associates with the community is in the vanguard of a movement for improvement of the entire society.

Those who identify themselves with this campaign rise above selfishness and concern only with self. They heed Hillel's admonition to be concerned with others as well as themselves. The Jewish Welfare Fund Campaign represents a miracle—the miracle of people striving together, strengthening each other to build a community and to bring forth a better life for all.

MULTIPLE APPEALS:
AN IMPEDIMENT TO ADVANCEMENT

Presented at the General Assembly of the Council of
Jewish Federations in Detroit
November 1980

In his keynote address to the 1980 General Assembly, the President of the Council of Jewish Federations spoke of a climate of cooperation among people, agencies, and groups in our communities. He described strong links between communities and major Jewish agencies and the need for the constant nourishing of these ties as well as our bridges to Israel. He emphasized the need for federations to raise one billion dollars by 1985, twice our present achievement.

That is what this is about—the need for more money and the unity required to obtain it. The Council President stated that with a real commitment to unity—not just in words, but in deeds—and genuine cooperation among agencies, groups, and people concerned with the well-being of all of Jewish life, we can achieve our billion dollar goal.

RESOLUTIONS OF THE PAST

In 1949, the General Assembly of this Council passed a resolution on the role of federations and their relationships to independent campaigns. This resolution stressed the importance of unified fundraising as follows: "In view of the discussions concerning fundraising and current problems facing the communities, this Assembly reaffirms the basic principle that all valid Jewish appeals deserving the support of the full Jewish community belong in the local Jewish Welfare Fund, except when there is mutual agreement between the Welfare Fund and the appeal, in which case the latter shall conduct its own campaign, and in such event the timing and other conditions governing such campaigns shall be worked out in agreement with the Welfare Funds."

That principle, the unification of fundraising, is basic to the very being of federations and the Jewish community. The Jewish community is dependent primarily upon two things: unified fundraising and unified planning. Disunity in fundraising creates obstacles to solid community planning.

The resolution went on to express concern with what was described as a multiplicity of campaigns. It stated, "Multiplicity is a serious threat to the capacity of the American Jewish community to meet the tremendous needs, local, national and overseas." It called upon the Council to work with appropriate agencies operating in America on behalf of Israel to prevent unnecessary and duplicated campaigns and to coordinate and merge related campaigns.

In succeeding General Assemblies, more resolutions were adopted as follows:

- 1959: A resolution noted that "CJFWF was instrumental several years ago in helping to bring about the establishment of the Committee on Authorization of Campaigns of the Jewish Agency for Israel. That committee has served to prevent a number of appeals from coming to communities and thereby to defuse the diversion of funds from Israel's most urgent needs."

The resolution then dealt with the plethora of efforts by what were described as "traditional institutions" and the need to deal with them intelligently.

- 1960: This resolution noted that the "American Jewish community is faced with needs of great urgency and magnitude, nationally, locally and overseas. Facts brought to this Assembly reflect substantial and growing independent fundraising in many fields of service. Involved is supplementary fundraising by some beneficiaries of Welfare Funds" (at times in violation of their agreements with Welfare Funds).

"We recognize that while Jewish Welfare Funds do not raise nor attempt to raise all funds in the Jewish community, they are concerned that maximum funds be raised and made available for agencies in relation to the relative urgency of their needs."

The resolution then went on to call upon communities to (1) systematically examine fundraising—in other words, to examine their practices in terms of inclusion or exclusion of a cause and an agency; (2) educate and encourage leaders and givers to consult the federation before accepting responsibility or contributing to individual drives; and (3) create statements of principles to deal with independent fundraising.

A Jewish Agency resolution passed in May 1973 stated, "The Agency should utilize the emergency campaign committee of the Israel government and the Agency to carry out responsibilities." It called upon all institutions and organizations in Israel to clear their plans in advance and not to sponsor or endorse campaigns without clearance. It emphasized the role of the Committee on Control and Authorization of Campaigns.

This was preceded by a February 1973 Jewish Agency resolution affirming the centrality, primacy, and priority of the Keren Hayesod, United Israel Appeal, and United Jewish Appeal.

In 1975, the CJFWF created a Task Force on Multiple Appeals. The next year, the task force issued a call for order in fundraising and announced its guidelines.

I recently examined again all of these guidelines, as well as all of the work done on the issue of multiple appeals. Had all these papers been put together and brought to the General Assembly (GA), they could have been sufficient to fill the packets given to the hundreds of GA participants.

Supplementary and multiple appeals have been a problem for a long time. They represent a contradiction of every resolution I have ever read and the very idea of Jewish community and federation. Many campaigns take place against a backdrop of tension within a community, without federation approval. Others obtain a grudging assent by federations reluctant to deal with the tensions produced by the denial of clearance, despite the confusion created by a multiplicity of efforts.

I live in a city in which there is relative order and cooperation, where the idea of community is strong, where people, by and large, work for the common good. It is that sense of unity of purpose that made it possible for us to pick up the remnants of our people and to help them live again and that gave us the strength to aid the people of Israel in 1948, 1967, 1973, and in other critical times. It is that deep feeling of mutual interest that enhances our passion for peoplehood.

Federation is a very sophisticated idea. It means not person against person, but person together with person. A community means people planning services together, to meet needs wherever they exist and, in unity, raising the funds with which to do the job. The federation is the central instrument through which the people of a community collaborate to meet needs.

UNIFYING FUNDRAISING

The resolutions cited earlier called upon communities to create statements of principles on unified fundraising, and many of them have. In some cities such principles are established policy and reinforce a oneness of purpose. In my own city such a statement, **Principles on Unified and Coordinated Fundraising,** has become policy overseen by an active, effective committee. There has not been one campaign for funds without federation agreement since those principles were adopted in 1957 and the committee was created. Of course, there has been some fundraising done apart from the federation for worthwhile things of special concern to a particular group but not deemed to be appropriate for funding by the entire community. In such instances, the federation and individual organizations determine the conditions of the campaign together (i.e., the fundraising goal, campaign methods, timing, and all other relevant matters).

In addition, because community planning is virtually synchronized with fundraising, no agency has initiated any new service without agreement by the Federation/Community Committee, the Central Planning Committee for Jewish Services.

Not all communities have adopted such policies. Some have passed resolutions that, without diligent application, remain only words. I have observed that some communities that have passed such resolutions have the biggest problems with multiple appeals. It is one thing to create a statement; it is another thing to apply it in an effective diplomatic way. Where such policies exist, constant vigilance is required in application of them.

Policies on unified and coordinated fundraising include special obligations for members of the federation's Board of Directors who must, "by virtue of the trust placed in them—provide leadership—in abiding by such principles" by associating themselves "only with fundraising activities of events, specifically cleared by the federation."

However, in some communities, board members are among those who violate these policies. Even some people who have held leading positions in the CJF behave in this way. Some key leaders of the United Jewish Appeal are party to overt competition by Israel-based organizations without federation clearance. Some officials of the State of Israel endorse fundraising efforts without understanding the implications for community campaigns that finance services in Israel.

MULTIPLE APPEALS ARE INIMICAL TO THE FEDERATION IDEAL

Federations came into being at the turn of the 20th century because it was good business. People had to protect themselves from constant solicitations. They settled on the idea of unifying fundraising for a variety of services and needs into one central fund and asked people to give the greatest possible sum of money to a single campaign. Leaders and workers of worthwhile organizations deserving full Jewish support unified their campaign into one, requiring their best efforts. And then time went by and we learned of the wisdom of examining needs together in advance of raising money, and the idea of community planning was born.

Multiple undisciplined campaigning is inimical to the obvious good common sense of unity. It means competition, not cooperation—disunity rather than community. It bewilders givers, confuses campaign workers, burdens professional staff members and executives, and troubles responsible board members, the community's decision makers.

Why the Problem?

Those who seek order and cooperativeness and unity know full well that these qualities do not attract all people. Professional fundraisers know that too. They know that some simply do not understand the sophisticated idea of community and federation. They know that a free market existing with agencies going in their own individual ways will have special appeal to some people, particularly the following types:

- those who want to be big fish in small ponds
- those who do not work, give, or lead effectively enough to become federation leaders, yet seek places in the sun
- those who buy leadership at bargain basement rates through a particularistic organization
- those who are flattered by public notice, honors, and plaques

I hasten to add that some people deserve special recognition and that plaques and awards are appropriate, if given selectively. My concern is directed at the misuse of such devices, which makes them destructive.

The Giver

The multiplicity of campaigns confuses givers. Let's place ourselves into the giver's position. Many individual organizations that make claims of helping Israel—often replicating the defined missions of the United Jewish Appeal—the Jewish Agency for Israel, and the United Israel Appeal, make appeals. The giver is told by various groups that they solve issues of human relations for Jews in America and around the world and sometimes that they strengthen Jewish culture or education with the money they raise. Claims by one organization duplicate the claims of another and still another so that the giver cannot tell them apart. The enlightened reader of the Anglo-Jewish press and the Jewish Telegraphic Agency Daily Report is struck by the extraordinary marketing of services by individual organizations and by unproved claims of achievement and worth on the part of national, overseas, and local agencies. Most of us are able to be fairly analytic about these claims, for as leaders of federations, volunteer and professional, we are expected to know about agencies and needs. But how does the individual donor differentiate the real from the contrived, the worthy from the unworthy?

The Worker

What of the worker? With a proliferation of appeals, workers are good people asked to work once, twice, three times and to solicit endlessly, in limitless efforts to accomplish what could be done in one big, well-coordinated campaign. Campaigns compete for and waste their time. Coordination means not just savings in terms of campaign costs; it means people working together, not against each other. It means the productive use of time, and time is life.

Campaign Professionals

Campaign professionals know fundraising techniques; they also know how to mount campaigns over federation opposition and even how to mobilize ventures to weaken the federation so that it cannot impede their efforts. Often, these ensuing conflicts mean less money for federation and therefore, for the legitimate services it finances.

Fundraising techniques that have the effect of splintering the community have become commonplace. The growing use of these techniques can be traced partly to how fundraisers are paid: the success of many professional fundraisers is measured only by the amount of money raised—which is a prime factor in determining their compensation.

Let us look at a few of these techniques:

- **The Steal the March Technique**: An organization that knows that the federation would not approve of an independent campaign does not ask the federation for clearance. Instead, it organizes a committee quietly and offers the community and the federation a fait accompli. It knows that federation opposition would create tension and that federations seek unity and harmony and are reluctant to rock the boat.

- **The Testimonial Dinner**: The testimonial dinner is often used as a technique to overcome objection by the federation. An organization that wishes to violate unifying community principles generally selects someone of influence to honor, preferably a very large giver to whom it is expected the federation would be deferential. Invitees to such an event assume the honoree to be devoted to the mission of the sponsoring organization, for why else would the organization have selected him or her? And yet, often the honoree has little if any involvement with the organization involved and has been selected because he or she is a person of means and influence whom people would want to or may need to please.

It is commonplace for a person given the role of honoree to protest with humility, real or feigned, stressing a lack of a need to be honored. But then nearly everyone needs a bit of recognition sometimes. Flattery can be a useful tool. As Jonathan Swift put it in a couplet long ago,

Flattery's the food of fools
Yet now and then your men of wit
Will condescend to take a bit

The honoree explains to others in a self-effacing way that he or she took on the role just to be helpful.

Fundraisers almost invariably expect the honoree to make a sizable gift, like a quid pro quo. People serve on the committee for the event, some in good humor and some quite reluctantly, and make gifts they otherwise would not make. Where the honoree is a major force in the business or social life of the community, someone people feel they must please, some participants make their presence conspicuous at the event as well as their gifts. The frequently affected humility of the honoree at such events reminds me of a comment a few years ago made by Golda Meir to a man who acted in this way. She told him, "Don't be so humble, you're not that great."

This is not to say that testimonial dinners do not have their place. However, when honors are bestowed on those who are not the most honorable and when these dinners are held in endless numbers, then they denigrate the idea of honor and splinter the community. The most hurtful of such fundraising efforts are ones carried out by organizations of little worth—sometimes by ones that the federation/community has carefully studied and decided not to support.

It should be stressed that this discussion is germane only to federation agencies and does not include the Israel Bonds effort for which testimonial events are standard procedure.

- **Misunderstanding Approach:** In this technique, the fundraising professional implies that the federation director or president has said the campaign was cleared. When that is denied by the federation, the worker then apologetically indicates that there must have been some misunderstanding and he or she learned of the objection to the campaign only after it was too late to stop it.

- **Memberships:** Another approach is not to have a campaign at all, but instead confine the procurement of money to the members of the organization. But before doing so, it is necessary to increase the size of the membership by making the fee nominal and ensuring that people of substantial means join. Then one should establish special categories of membership—$100, $400, $5,000, $50,000—whatever the traffic will bear. Finally, fundraising is limited to the membership, but be certain that it is a sizable membership with a lot of money.

- **Honor the Non-Jew Approach:** Relatively new, the honor the non-Jew approach means selection of a non-Jew of substance as an honoree. Fundraisers know that all too often Jews will feel that they must respond, lest a lack of response sparks a negative reaction from non-Jews. They also feel obligated to respond to return the goodwill of the non-Jewish honoree and other non-Jewish participants who may have been on a committee. All too frequently non-Jews who are approached feel they must also participate or else be regarded somehow as anti-Semitic. Tensions, whether overtly expressed or opaque, often result.

  Certainly, a Jewish community and/or Jewish organizations may honor non-Jews who make extraordinary contributions to the well-being of humankind and more specifically to the Jewish people. Yet, the current trend toward gimmickry in the use of this approach is often demeaning of the community and of honorees who are so used.

There is a new trend in some communities to make lump sum allocations to a local agency and then charge it with the responsibility for raising money to meet the rest of its needs. That is precisely contrary to the basic objective and meaning of the resolution of 1949, which stated "that all valid Jewish appeals deserving the support of the full Jewish community belong in the local Jewish Welfare Fund." Federations using such approaches do a disservice to the very essence of federation, to the philosophy of people working together to meet shared needs. This approach can easily become self-defeating as often it results in major giving to specific organizations with which people are associated and reduced giving to the federation. It demeans the community.

Some people can see only the particular things with which they are concerned, things that are visible and within reach. However, if everyone works for a favorite cause in competition with every other person, we have the antithesis of community. The federation is a concept through which we address ourselves to the welfare of all people and to the problems and needs of the whole community at one time. Groups and people cannot survive well as islands. Jewish life does not thrive that way.

The Federation Executive

Professional fundraisers know how to implement fundraising methods, but so does any intelligent federation executive. The federation executive should also be expected to anticipate and to have vision, which is the art of seeing what may not be visible to others. He or she knows that a lack of unity in fundraising is disruptive. The competent federation professional helps develop a responsible volunteer leadership with whom to create a community spirit. That mood leads to a community culture in which those who lead are constructive examples for others. Example is the school of humankind. People learn more through example than through any other means.

Astute federation executives keep their ears to the ground; they know what's going on. Often in a place where the spirit of community has eroded, they tell themselves a little white lie to reassure themselves as well as others that all is well. They may say, "The federation wouldn't get the money anyway" and "it doesn't matter," but in truth, it does.

There is something glorious about a community, something elevating about a federation when people come together in unity, in which problems are best solved not by any individual or individual group but by the community/federation. Competition between organizations, local, national, or international, represents a form of banalization of the Jewish community and a coarsening of Jewish communal service. The future of the united community is bright, but the future of a place where there is a multiplicity of particu-laristic campaigns, inevitably leading to disunity, is dim.

It is time now to stop passing resolutions. It is time for men and women of goodwill to work together to achieve common objectives, to live and build together. It is time for leaders of communities to join together in federations and for federations to work together, as well as the Council of Jewish Federations, the United Jewish Appeal, and the Jewish Agency for Israel, to truly federate continental and international fundraising. Then our target can be a billion dollars. If we work together and live together, our goal will be achieved.

CAMPAIGN CHALLENGES

Synopsis of a talk given to the Campaign Technical Advisory Committee of the Council of Jewish Federations, federation executives, and campaign chairs in New York.

December 1962

Every federation executive and campaign director knows two things: how tough it is to raise money and that the community never raises sufficient funds to meet its needs.

Every year, we resolve to review our campaign structures; organize early; campaign aggressively; bring new leadership into the campaign; orient the workers effectively; market the campaigns properly; and individualize solicitations, particularly of larger givers who provide the most money.

To evaluate past fundraising efforts, it is helpful for each of us to ask these questions:

- How strong is your community?
- To what extent is the federation understood and accepted within the community?
- Does the federation's day by day works create confidence in it as an effective centralized community instrument?
- To what extent does the federation have the strength to obtain cooperation from all elements in the community?
- Are the people who lead the federation respected bona fide community leaders?
- To what extent do members of the federation's Board of Directors

demonstrate real commitment to the federation idea?

- Has the federation been producing new leaders and young leaders able to build the future?

- To what extent is there unified and coordinated fundraising in our communities?

- To what extent have we recruited workers on the basis of their skills and their commitment to the ideals we represent?

- To what extent have we intensified the programs of worker education and orientation so workers understand what they represent and grow in confidence in telling this campaign story unreservedly?

- To what extent do we exercise care in matching the solicitors and solicitees?

- To what extend do we understand the giving capacities of people so that we may use discretion in what is asked of them?

In Ecclesiastes, we read "there's nothing new under the sun." There's hardly anything new in campaigning. Shortcuts to success do not exist.

Campaign—A Unifying Force

The federation campaign is the largest, most visible undertaking within each Jewish community. Although its function is to raise money—a lot of money—its outcome is another significant byproduct: it brings together people of all views in a common cause. Properly conducted, the campaign is an agent in developing a spirit of community/federation. In communities in which such primacy is not achieved, campaign results inevitably suffer.

I work in a community that has been comparatively successful during the last several years. The 1962 campaign result represents an increase of 92% over the campaign valley of 1955. The community achieves success by adhering to these guidelines:

- Stress the primacy of the welfare fund campaign, creating a mood intolerant of a multitude of appeals.

- Coordinate fundraising, protecting the giver from unnecessary, unwise, and often wasteful fundraising efforts.

- Place emphasis on the quality as well as quantity of workers—by studying the records of workers and tactfully avoiding assignments to unproductive ones.

- Conduct an annual review of givers; assign responsibility for those whose gifts are fixed and seem immutable in ways that will command less time but concentrate the work of the best workers on the givers with the greatest potential giving power—people who must be seen face to face.

- Streamline the campaign, discarding ineffective divisions; like trades and professional groups, which we felt functioned like mutual protective societies.

- Team solicitation—two workers together seeing the giver. One person is a worker; two is a committee representing the community.

- Intensify worker education and training.

- Solicit nearly all gifts in advance of campaign functions, using the function as a target date for conclusion and improvement of giving.

- Stress the women's division, the warmth it adds and its influence not only through gifts but the effect of participation by women on husbands, and children.

Emergency or Special Funds

The word "emergency" has become a trap. Used each year, it has become synonymous with "business as usual." But in truth, emergency conditions have been a constant for Israel and for the Jewish world for several decades. Any community that attempts to sell the special fund as a single-year expression of alarm errs.

It is time for us to set aside the term "special" or "emergency" and make it understood that the special character of our campaigns is always an emergency, requiring that people become accustomed to giving the maximum amount of money they are capable of at any given time.

Economic Factors

Economic factors, do of course affect the campaign, but let's recognize that most large givers are relatively secure financially and that few give amounts near to their capacities. The best evidence of that is the great disparity in giving levels by people who are in the same general economic brackets. Differences result from emotional makeup, the extent to which they are able to be concerned with others as well as themselves, and the depth of their identification with Jewish life. In 1946 the American Jewish community raised far more money than every before. People were shaken by what had occurred in the Holocaust, the problems of survivors, and the displaced persons camps. Yet, in 1948 the campaign results far exceeded that of 1946 because people gave with heart as well as mind.

Future tax code changes may reduce tax-deductible benefits for philanthropic gifts. But I don't believe we have cause for fear. We know that few of our givers have ever taken full advantage of the cooperation afforded by the government in permitting allowances for gifts to philanthropy. And let's remember that Jews were giving substantial amounts to philanthropic causes before 1913 when income tax laws came into effect permitting deductions for giving.

Goal Setting

Some communities establish goals related to what they believe is a realizable figure with a view that unattained goals would negatively affect the morale of campaign workers, creating a sense of defeat.

The Milwaukee Jewish community has not reached a campaign goal since 1946. In the monumental campaign effort of 1948, when the impressive amount of $1,750,000 was raised, the goal was, in fact, $2,500,000. In 1962, the goal was $1,750,000. The result will be approximately $1,500,000 and there will be no feeling of defeat. Our goals are set not on the basis of what we expect to achieve, but rather on what we estimate the needs to be. We tell the members of the community what the needs are, and we ask them to collectively share in reaching it. We believe that we behave with greater integrity in telling the people what the needs are and celebrating a satisfactory achievement. That is preferable to setting an easily reachable goal far short of real needs in order to celebrate a hollow achievement.

Some communities depend on advertising and public media to a greater degree than others. I do believe that ads buttress the campaign and may possibly encourage campaign workers in their efforts. But I've yet to see one piece of advertising from any source and in any media that in itself makes a great deal of difference. We cannot ever be dependent on a barrage of advertising. The times in which people gave because of front-page headlines, sensationalized news, or great claims to accomplishment have passed. The future requires more understanding on the part of community members in face-to-face discussion, not just selling but interpretation and education.

One Community—One Central Campaign

The federation is a community's central Jewish, communal organization. Yet, the idea of central organization is not fully accepted. Some speak of the support of the federation for a few weeks during the spring and ignore it the rest of the year. Some give lip service to what we represent, but then express fear that the organization that they most favor may lose autonomy. Some mount fundraising efforts for individual organizations in which a gift of modest size produces high status. Some people need to be big fish in small ponds.

Any campaign for funds, for whatever purpose, has an effect upon other efforts including those encompassed within the federation. I suggest in the strongest possible terms that those communities that do not now have specific methods for clearing campaigns by individual organizations and for developing order should hasten to develop such procedures. Applying such principles will create stress for voluntary leaders and for professionals, particularly executives of federations. But doing so represents principled conduct.

Campaign Leadership

No one can serve as a campaign chairman forever. The workers can have long tenure, but there will always be a need for new workers to succeed the veterans. We need to retain the prestige of the seasoned leader while bringing in new recruits to help shoulder the burdens.

We also need to widen the base of leadership. A study in 1954 in my own community brought to light that approximately 500 positions of leadership (i.e., membership on all of the boards of directors of the communal agencies and major committees of the federation or the Welfare Fund) were held by 150

people, two-thirds of whom were members of one synagogue. That is a plain-
ly undesirable situation. It is now changed so that all elements of the community are invited in and the involvement of all will grow in quality and improve
in quantity.

Campaigning is hard work for voluntary workers and for professionals. My
own observation of workers is that many are quite fearful of the job of solicitation. Asking people for money can be most trying, but when the task is assigned
to uninspired people without knowledge, it becomes all the more difficult.

Good training methods can make the difference between ruthless and zeal-
ous campaign work. Intensive education can only be done well in small
groups, preferably in the homes of workers themselves. In Milwaukee, training processes, instituted by our Women's Division and then adopted for all
campaign workers, have paid great dividends, creating a group spirit, contributing to a sense of commitment, and strengthening the confidence of
workers in their capacities to achieve good results. They depend on a system
using group dynamics, now in standard use for all campaign divisions and
which has been adapted in many many communities.

Campaigns within a Campaign

Leaders must lead in a campaign. The campaign leader cannot in good
conscience ask others to make commitments without him- or herself serving
as a model. In a study of 1,200 campaign workers in Milwaukee a year ago, we
found a strong correlation between the level of giving by the worker and his
or her effectiveness in obtaining suitable gifts from other donors. A worker
whose gift represents a sacrifice and who identifies with the federation agencies will work well with donors.

In a paper delivered in 1961, Henry Zucker noted that the board of directors
of the Cleveland Federation had in the 1960 campaign given about 20% of the
total money raised. In a similar study, giving by board members in Milwaukee
in 1962 represented 21% of the campaign total. The gifts of people who serve
on the boards of directors of all communal agencies encompassed in the federation campaign including the federation itself gave 41% of all money raised
in 1962. It is now our intent to conduct a campaign within a campaign among

board members, people who serve on the boards of local chapters of national organizations.

This approach has a usefulness that goes beyond campaigning itself. It is in effect preparation for a budgeting process. It conveys to people in advance that the amount of funds available to support agencies with which they are involved and in which they have a particularistic interest depends upon the campaign results and that they are themselves responsible for that achievement. It leads to understanding on the part of people that if there is a shortfall that they are themselves responsible. It makes clear that the budget is related to campaign results as well as to community planning to determine needs.

The Immediate Future

In next year's campaign, it is important that we do the following:

1. Establish a procedure for intensive examination of the giving records of donors long in advance, so that people may be placed into suitable categories for prospective giving. Often, campaign professionals and leaders find resistance to such work among some cynics, who insist because donors are well known that there is no need to review their giving records. In my community, small groups meeting over a period of several weeks have upgraded and shifted people from division to division. The procedure resulted in an impressive rate of increase. We do it every year.

2. Follow the rule that the dedicated worker is a dedicated giver—that workers give first, becoming the pacesetters and that they are joined in leading the way by board members of the federation itself and its partner agencies.

3. Create a more intensive process of education for workers.

4. Avoid big meetings for solicitation purpose, except as culminating affairs.

5. Establish the primacy of the campaign, and educate members of the community about needs involved and reasons for federation campaign priority.

6. Concentrate the campaign into a briefer period in which a level of substantial excitement can be ongoing.

As Jews, we have a special obligation to help other Jews. We can do that
effectively only if our federations are strong and for that they must have good
campaigns.

ADVANCING SOCIAL PLANNING IN MILWAUKEE

Adapted from an article in *Jewish Social Services Quarterly*
co-authored with Elkan C. Voorsanger
March, 1949

Federations developed out of the need to unify fundraising; the need for coordinated social planning has been harder for community members to accept. It has taken nearly ten years to interpret to the Milwaukee Jewish community the fact that the federation, the central communal organization, is responsible for both fundraising activities and the social planning of the community. Many "unmet needs" in the community have remained "unmet" not only because of our preoccupation with the critical overseas needs of the past fifteen years but also because there was no definite and continuous program of planning.

For the last four years we have had an active Central Planning Committee that has devoted itself to conducting numerous studies and to solving pressing and at times critical community problems. Acceptance on the part of the various agencies involved has in the main been most satisfactory, and progress in understanding both the program and function of the planning body has been achieved. However, interpretation of its mission to the general community and the community's subsequent understanding of the function of centralized social planning have been somewhat slower. Yet, visible signs of real progress are becoming increasingly evident. Implementation of some of the studies that have already been conducted has taken place, and we are on the verge of accomplishing major projects for the community. Now we have reached the point at which we can look forward to more than leisurely progress.

CENTRAL PLANNING COMMITTEE FOR JEWISH SERVICES

We think we have demonstrated to our cooperating agencies the obvious fact that cooperative action between social agencies is a basic ingredient of community progress. The lay leaders and executives who are involved in the work of our Central Planning Committee are evidencing a real cooperation and have helped bring about a healthy approach to the problem of social planning.

In this brief description of central planning for social services we do not mean to give the impression that there had been no centralized action of any kind in the community. Even during the years when fundraising was the major focus, coordination and orderliness had been achieved in the fields of civic protection through the Milwaukee Jewish Council, service to immigrants through the Milwaukee Committee for Jewish Refugees, and education through the newly established bureau of Jewish Education. Eventually it is hoped that these services as well as all other community activities will be planned through the Central Planning Committee and that each and every local community problem will be processed through it.

When the Central Planning Committee was finally established in 1945, it came as the logical culmination of discussions initiated by the federation with the functional agencies. These deliberations had resulted in the general agreement that a permanent body would be developed through which the agencies could work together, where each could have the guidance of others and the strengths of all could be combined to deal with problems of common concern.

The Central Planning Committee for Jewish Services was developed as the social planning arm of the federation and the total Jewish community. Its purposes have been defined in very broad general terms as being "analyzing various community services and agencies to determine relationships which they bear to each other; the uncovering of unmet needs in the community; planning for the solution of problems and interpreting agencies' programs, needs and objectives to the general community."

Agencies that have voluntarily associated themselves with the central planning body include the Mt. Sinai Hospital, Jewish Community Center, Jewish Family and Children's Service (which represents a merger of the Jewish Social Service Association and the Milwaukee Jewish Children's Home), Jewish Vocational Service, and the Children's Outing Association. The Home for Aged Jews and the Jewish Convalescent Home are not yet full affiliates, but have chosen to send observers to attend meetings, participate in social planning activity, and generally serve as liaison between their agencies and the Central Planning Committee.

The Central Planning Committee provides the agencies with an opportunity to become better acquainted with each other and, more important, to relate their problems and work each to the other. Decisions reached by the planning body are frequently the result of compromise between opposing views. Unity of decision is reached after study, full discussion, and eventual acceptance of the point of view of the committee. Final decisions are never arbitrarily arrived at. We are satisfied when compromises can be effected so that major differences can be resolved to the benefit of the total community. It is our conviction that we have a mechanism to attack and modify those differences that deprive the community of adequate service.

There are no standing subcommittees of the main central planning body with the exception of the Executive Committee, which is responsible for operation of the organization between meetings of the delegates. Social planning activity is carried on through subcommittees appointed as required by specific problems. On these subcommittees sit lay and professional representatives selected from the committee membership and the community at large. The study of a problem may be initiated at the request of any individual agency or member of the committee. Subcommittees are responsible for fact-finding, analysis, discussion, and recommendations regarding the problem studied. The recommendations of subcommittees are submitted to the full planning body for action. The decisions of the Central Planning Committee are communicated to participating agencies and constitute recommendations to them, with the responsibility for carrying out these recommendations being left to the agencies.

Although the complete autonomy of these agencies has meant they are free to accept or reject such recommendations, a moral obligation to accept, or at least not to disregard recommendations without requesting reconsideration by the planning body, has seemed to take hold. Possibly this stems from the fact that each agency participates in the discussions reached and has an opportunity to express its thinking in the deliberations. At the same time the right of agencies to accept or reject recommendations has sometimes resulted in at least a temporary lag in action and progress.

STUDIES – SURVEYS – PLANNING

Projects and studies undertaken include an overall health survey of the Jewish community, which examined needs for health and medical service, the ability of the existing facilities to meet these needs, the place of a Jewish hospital, and the responsibility of the Jewish community to provide such facilities. This survey, which is being directed by Dr. J. J. Golub of New York, is now reaching its conclusion, and through the Central Planning Committee it will provide the community with a blueprint for the extension of medical facilities, methods of meeting health needs, and the relationship that each agency, which provides such service, should bear to one another. The central planning body has also studied, made recommendations, and placed responsibility for a scholarship program in the community, the purpose of which is to equalize opportunity for education and training for those people who might otherwise not have opportunities for realizing their full potential. The Central Planning Committee has studied and made recommendations in regard to needs for Jewish nursery schools and Jewish communal responsibility for meeting these needs. It has established responsibility for financial assistance and service to the chronically ill. Projects that may soon be underway include a study of relationships between the casework and vocational agencies and a study of the group work program of the community. Additional projects have received attention and are under consideration, all in an effort to achieve a healthy Jewish community.

Our Central Planning Committee has successfully obtained cooperation among various organizations on a level beyond anything previously known.

The procurement of such cooperation is especially significant when we note the varying Federation-Community Chest relationships of the agencies; some are financed entirely or in part by the federation, others in part or entirely by the Community Fund, and two of them, namely the Home for the Aged and the Convalescent Home, receive no funds from central organizations. Whether expressed by them or not, the association of functional agencies within the social planning arm of the federation indicates a recognition on the part of each that it is responsible not only to itself but in a broad sense to the entire community through the central communal organization. The federation's acceptance of responsibility for central planning represents complete recognition on its part that it bears a responsibility for assuring the community and its members of adequate services to meet existing and future needs. It represents further a joint recognition on the part of functional agencies and the federation that there can be only one central organization in the community responsible for fundraising, financing, community organization, and planning.

Although the definitely voluntary nature of our planning body may stem partially from the caution of agencies in giving up any autonomy, it is also based on the recognition that it is the only method that can be successful at the present time. It is, therefore, our purpose to bring about a closer and stronger voluntary association, ready at all times to take unified action, based on full discussion, mediation, and frequently compromise. At the same time, we must face the reality that the voluntary nature of the association and the inherent privilege of agencies to accept or reject recommendations may eventually require structural changes. We wonder whether the future may not require some sacrifice of autonomy in the name of more effective community planning for social welfare.

After having achieved some measure of growth and success in our program, we have arrived at the point where we feel that a stock-taking of the activities and operation of our Central Planning Committee is necessary. Therefore, at the present time we are engaged in a review of our structure and our program. We are hopeful that the example of the central body may be a stimulus toward a periodic examination by the cooperating agencies of their services.

Part II:
The Jewish World

An Introductory Word

At the request of the Joint Distribution Committee, HIAS, the Council of Jewish Federations, and the Jewish Agency for Israel, the Milwaukee Federation allowed me the time from work to serve as a consultant to several Jewish communities around the world. From 1962 and continuing for many years after my retirement in 1984, I served as a consultant to Brazil and other countries in South America, the European Council of Jewish Communities, various countries in Europe, Israel, and communities in Canada, as well as in the United States.

In addition, executives and voluntary leaders of Brazil, Belgium, and other countries came to Milwaukee to study community organization activity for training and leadership development purposes. Officers who were about to retire from the Israel Defense Forces, and were selected to serve as executives of Jewish communities in other countries including South Africa, also came to Milwaukee for training purposes.

The Growing Jewish Community of Brazil

Address to the Board of Directors and Executive Staffs of the American Jewish Joint Distribution Committee, Jewish Agency for Israel, and United HIAS Service. Given as a consultant to the Brazilian Jewish community

September 1962

A few years ago, a hippopotamus was elected as a deputy to the National Senate of Brazil. Please understand I am not writing metaphorically: a hippopotamus actually was a write-in candidate, and he received more votes than any other candidate representing the official parties of the largest state in Brazil. He did not, of course, actually assume office, and the Brazilian people were spared government by a hippopotamus. A literacy test is applied to public officials, and alas, our popular hippopotamus could not read. The election, however, reflected the political upheaval, economic chaos, and the contempt of Brazilians for officials who govern.

I confess that I was incredulous when I heard this story. Its true meaning is sadly indicative of the frustration, unhappiness, and cynicism of the Brazilians regarding their government.

South America is a seething continent. Many lands are governed by corrupt dictatorial regimes. In Peru, a military junta assumed power in July, driving the elected president out of the country. The legal president of Brazil, Frondizi, lives in involuntary exile on an island off the coast of Argentina, while his successor, Jose Mario Guido, a puppet of a corrupt army, strives ineptly to avoid another revolution. Last year, the duly elected president of Brazil, Janio Guadros, abruptly resigned his post after only eight months in office, and the country teetered on the verge of rebellion. However, Brazilians are peaceful and government takeovers are bloodless. An optimistic people, they have a saying, "Dios es un Brasileno"—"God is a Brazilian"—all will be well.

ECONOMIC SITUATION

Extraordinary wealth and grinding poverty live side by side in the subcontinent that is Brazil, a land larger than the continental United States. Illiteracy is taken for granted; only 16 million people in a population of 75 million are able to pass the literacy test required to vote. Two-thirds of sixth-grade children do not attend school. In July 1962, the farmers and peasants who produce food, which they themselves could not afford to buy, staged a series of revolts. The upper-class wealthy people fear the influence of Castro and Cuba and leftist political movements. Rampant corruption is taken for granted. It is the extraordinary individual who pays taxes in full.

The value of the Brazilian currency, the cruzero, has been deflated at a rate that challenges an American imagination. In 1948, an American visitor would have received 25 cruzeros for his dollar; in 1958, 80 cruzeros; in 1960, 198; and in August of 1962, the cruzero skyrocketed on one day to 780 for a dollar. With rampant inflation, prices increased by 50% last year. The minimum wage is a munificent $20 per month—in American terms. The average per capita income in 1960 was $240 per year, approximately one-tenth of the per capita income in the United States. Well-informed observers estimate that 90% of the wealth of Brazil is invested in other countries, despite the fact that it is illegal to send money out of Brazil. The inability of the country to husband its resources is marked by the fact that though it used to be first in the world in exports of cocoa and rubber, it is now third in cocoa and it must import rubber.

Despite economic and political disorder affecting masses of people, Brazil remains a land of opportunity for educated, skillful people of vision. It has great natural resources and large land areas to be developed, settled, and populated. It has welcomed large-scale immigration; 400,000 Japanese have come to the city of Sao Paulo alone since World War II. Italians, Germans, Chinese, French, Portuguese, and North Africans have come in search of opportunity. The doors have been open to Jewish immigration, and HIAS has resettled substantial numbers of immigrants who have helped build the nation of which they quickly become a part. Jewish immigrants have helped create great cities, like Rio and Sao Paulo; the latter city is a metropolitan area of over 5 million and described as the fastest-growing city in the world where construction is moving so rapidly it seems to fly on the wings of the wind.

THE JEWISH COMMUNITY OF BRAZIL

In Brazil there is a relatively modern Jewish community made up of cultured people who have come from lands that had become the graveyards of their brothers: Poland, Romania, Germany, Egypt, Morocco, Algeria, Syria, and Lebanon. There are even some immigrants from Israel. Bringing with them technical know-how, they become quickly acculturated into their new land. The Jewish community of Sao Paulo, Brazil's largest city, has grown from 20,000 in pre-Hitler times to 70,000 now. They are a free people, able to live as Jews and practice their religion.

But it was not always so. In the 15th century, Jews came to Brazil from Portugal and Spain in flight from the Inquisition. Some became new Christians, Marranos, but continued to covertly practice their Judaism. Later, under tolerant Dutch rule, synagogues sprung up. (Kahal Zur Israel, in Recife founded in 1637, is the first synagogue in the Americas, and it still stands on Rua Do Bon Jesus—Street of the Good Jesus). When the Portuguese re-conquered the territory, Jews fled to other Dutch colonies, such as the Antilles and New Amsterdam (1654), where they helped build the great Jewish community of New York. It was not until Brazil freed itself from Portugal that they could be Jews openly in Brazil. Now, there are approximately 100 synagogues throughout the country.

Growing Anti-Semitism

Today, South America is a major center for the Nazi movement. Anti-Semitic attacks intensified after SS Officer Adolf Eichmann was convicted and hanged in Ramleh prison in Israel on May 31, 1962. Synagogues and Jewish community buildings have been bombed and Jewish high-school students attacked. A young Jewish university student was kidnapped and driven to an isolated place where swastikas were carved on her body. On the day when my family and I were leaving Buenos Aires, a bomb, Molotov cocktails, and gunfire were used in three separate attacks on Jewish business enterprises in San Miguel, a suburb of Buenos Aires. Less than two weeks later, a Roman Catholic priest named Julio Meinvielle, the spiritual leader of Tacuara, a Nazi-style student organization that has been charged with anti-Semitic atrocities, told a New York Times correspondent that "Jews were striving to take over the riches of all peoples, to corrupt them and reduce them to the status of slaves." In language reflective of "The Protocols of the Elders of Zion," he described Jews as "an accursed race and agents and sons of the devil." Although other priests and church leaders condemned Father Meinvielle, he was able to use the Catholic university hall for a speech.

Despite assurances provided by President Jose Mario Guido and other members of his cabinet, there is fear that anti-Semitism will increase and that the Catholic Church may tolerate it. The Jewish bi-weekly newspaper, La Luz, reported that it was "no secret" that Nazi and Fascist organizations were spiritually led by priests, including Father Justo Oscar Laguna, notorious for his anti-Semitic sermons. There is fear that anti-Semitism, which has often been preceded by economic and social tensions, may increase as the discontent of hungry, uneducated people is easily converted to anger at the Jews, the historic scapegoats.

In Brazil, many homes of substance are surrounding by tall, iron fences, and well-to-do people employ armed guards to patrol the outside of their homes. This was true even of the homes of modestly affluent Jewish people, a possible harbinger of things to come in much of South America.

Yet the Jews of Brazil feel welcome. Brazilian Cardinal Don Vincente Scherer of Porto Alegre is reported to be giving full support to a Jewish request that the Catholic Church and the Vatican delete anti-Jewish material from Catholic teaching and liturgy during the second Vatican Council being convened by Pope John XXIII. Recently, Porto Alegre renamed a square as Herzl Square in honor of Theodore Herzl, founder of political Zionism. Colonel Isaac Nahon, a Sephardic Jew, was elevated to the rank of general and placed in command of a division of the Brazilian army, the third such promotion for a

Jew by the army during the last four months. Horatio Laufer, a Jew, was foreign minister under President Kubitschek de Oliveira (1956-61).

The constant threats in Argentina are producing a greater determination on the part of the Jewish community to resist attacks. Jewish passivity is diminishing; the ghetto psychology is fading. Most communities have developed a political agility in dealing with governments and the power structures of countries. Jewish communities have begun to collaborate with other minorities in seeking human rights.

Social Conditions in the Jewish Community

The Jewish people of Brazil, like newcomers to the United States, have created social organizations in which they can associate primarily with others of the same national origin; for example, there are clubs of German Jews, Poles, and Romanians. The approximately 5,000 Egyptians who have immigrated very recently maintain their separateness from people from other Muslim countries, such as Morocco, Algeria, and Syria. This exclusiveness may be expected to diminish with time. Just as the largest Jewish immigration to the United States from Eastern Europe was eventually accepted by the preceding German Jewish immigrants, who in turn had absorbed earlier Sephardic communities, so may a convergence of interests be expected to develop in Brazil.

There is a major difference between the Jewish people of Brazil and our ancestors in the United States, many of whom sought economic opportunities not available to them in the many European ghettos and shtetls so that we, their children, could live a better life. The Jewry of Brazil and South America is a cultured, sophisticated people who emigrated with many skills and much education. It is impressive to an American, who speaks few languages, to witness a group of people who swing freely from Portuguese to English, to German, to French, to Yiddish, to Spanish. There is an eloquence about the staff of an agency, who can converse in twelve languages, as I found in the office of United HIAS. It was staffed essentially by immigrants themselves, many of whom had experienced the loss of spouses, parents, and children and some bearing physical and emotional scars almost visible to the naked eye. The deep hurt such people have experienced, which will be part of them for all of their days, results in a devotion and readiness to serve newly arrived Jewish immigrants.

During the last few years, many thousands of new immigrants have flowed through the open doors of this country; 7,000 Jewish people arrived in Sao Paulo, 2,500 in 1957 alone. When compared to the reluctance of American Jewish communities to accept more immigrants, the readiness of the Brazilian Jewish community to accept their Jewish brethren is very impressive. Though people come with little, they are quickly independent.

A Communal Spirit Is Developing Slowly

Just as with the frenzied pace of the building boom in Sao Paulo in which a few structures collapsed because of careless planning, the Jewish community, in some ways seems to resemble this aspect of Brazilian life. Groups in the Jewish community interested in a particular kind of service simply build as they see fit. Buildings have been created without planning and without demonstrated need. Some substantial structures built by Jewish community groups stand unused and are symbols of waste, misdirection of energy, and planlessness. The separation of group from group results in duplication of efforts and waste. The American federation idea of coordinated services is new and not yet deeply rooted in Brazil. The concept of community, of planning and coordinating services, has yet to be learned. As occurred in the United States, this is an expensive lesson.

However, the Brazilian community is in the early stages of developing a communal group spirit. None of us in the United States expects to erase the depths of differences between religious groups, yet we recognize that there is room for difference in the minds of people. As we believe in unity without uniformity, the Brazilian Jewish community may be expected to learn these same lessons.

The Jews of Brazil are imbued with a love of Israel as a sense of Jewish peoplehood prevails. They consider themselves the partners of American Jews in supporting major international agencies, such as HIAS, the Jewish Agency for Israel, and the Joint Distribution Committee. In addition, they help world Jewry by absorbing refugees at a quick pace.

Yet, Brazilian Jews take fierce pride in being Brazilians. They resent strongly, as we do, any allegations in regard to their loyalty to their country, even as they simultaneously pursue a profound dedication to Israel as being at the core of Judaism.

Jewish Communal Agencies and Services

American professionals may consider most of the Brazilian Jewish social agencies that exist to be relatively unsophisticated, yet their work has effectively helped refugees to become self-sustaining in a short period of time.

Financial assistance is administered by the Conselho de Assistencia Social, supported by United HIAS, which reports the cost of such assistance as the lowest per capita in the world. The Conselho's employment bureau, staffed by only one person, placed 305 people in jobs in 1960. Of 157 people from Romania who arrived in 1960 with a median age of 51, one-half were placed in employment within three months and two-thirds within six, this despite the fact that these new immigrants had no knowledge of the Portuguese language prior to arrival. Their average income is considerably higher than the average income of most Brazilians of longer standing. Of the 141 families containing 324 people receiving assistance from the Conselho more than 50% required only nominal assistance for often short-term financial problems.

The director of one major Jewish institution supported in part by funds by an American international Jewish organization, is paid on a commission basis, (i.e., 10% of all of the institution's income), an unwise, potentially dangerous arrangement that could encourage unnecessary institutionalization of elderly people, which would increase income, financially benefiting the executive.

Other major local communal agencies are Vaad Hachinuch [Bureau of Jewish Education]; Linath Hatzdek [Outpatient Medical Clinic]; Ofidas [Women's and Children's Individual and Group Service Agency]; Ciam [School for Children with Learning Problems]; Lar das Velhos [Home for the Aged]; Lar das Criancas [Children's Home]; and Albert Einstein Hospital [currently being built]. There is also the Lan Kassa—a loan fund for refugees supported by Claims Conference money.

An outpatient medical and health clinic, the Poly Clinic, is an example of the need for coordination and planning. It is situated in a clean new building that was created without suitable study or planning to determine the true need for it and its potential usage. In a visit, I found many of its rooms completely unused. Yet, Ezra, an organization that provides help for men with individual and health problems, refused space in the Poly Clinic, preferring to be separate, and is in the process of creating its own new building. Leading community members view the Ezra organization as being led by people of limited vision, narrow in purpose, and primarily concerned with bringing credit to their organization. Ofidas provides medical services for women and children separately. Thus, members of the same family are served by three different agencies. The need for communal planning and cooperation is very evident.

The director of HIAS has taken the initiative in developing a council of professionals of the various communal agencies. Regular meetings of this council in which there is an exchange of information and ideas are enhancing cooperation. Many of these professionals are graduates of the local school of social work; some would unquestionably benefit from graduate school training in the United States.

The federation, an overall representative body of the Jewish community, is made up of people designated by 54 organizations, inclusive of all synagogues, social, and welfare organizations. Created in 1947, the federation is respected as an idea, but its time has not truly yet come. Though it conducts an annual campaign for funds to support agencies, most of the agencies raise as much funds from separate campaigns as they receive from the federation, which is unable currently to coordinate services.

The Magbit, the united fundraising campaign, has three major partners—the federation, the Keren Hayesod, and the Zionist organization. During the last several years, campaign proceeds have been divided in accordance with this formula: 70 percent for the Keren Hayesod in Israel and 30 percent for the federation for local services, including programs for refugees. The Magbit has made available a special subvention to the federation to be used for United HIAS programs for refugees. From an emergency rescue fund conducted in 1962 for the Keren Hayesod, 10 percent of the funds raised were allocated to the Joint Distribution Committee.

RECOMMENDATIONS FOR STRENGTHENING THE BRAZILIAN JEWISH COMMUNITY

These recommendations are offered for consideration by HIAS, the Council of Jewish Federations, the JDC, the Jewish Agency for Israel, and responsible decision makers in Brazil. Though nothing can be imposed on Sao Paulo, I believe they would be acceptable to the leaders of the community.

1. **Federation:** Sao Paulo should have one single central Jewish organization responsible for communal planning, budgeting, and fundraising. The Magbit and the federation should be merged into the one central entity, which should be governed by a board of directors consisting of representatives of the total community as well as some designated by the various agencies. Such a central instrument would be useful in increasing cooperation and enhancing a sense of community among groups with particularistic interests.

2. **Buildings:** Creation of new buildings should be discouraged during the period of development of the new central organization. It would be difficult to achieve a complete building moratorium, but every effort should be exerted to avoid compounding the errors previously made. Any future construction should await a suitable study of needs and careful planning.

3. **Jewish Community Center:** The lack of a JCC is a major gap in services, and planning and building one should be a major priority. The very process of consideration of the values of a JCC and its eventual construction would help bring various groups together, thereby diminishing the insularity and separation of group from group.

4. **Fundraising:** The new central organization should conduct a united campaign embracing all causes deemed to be the responsibility of the total community. A more unified effort can be expected to raise more money and result in better financial support than is currently possible. There is a clear need for an experienced, professional campaign director who would help introduce more sophisticated fundraising methods and concepts.

5. **A Women's Division:** The present second-class role of women and their lack of presence in leadership roles in agencies, including the Magbit, deprive the community of a great reservoir of leadership. Where women are involved along with men in governance, the work of agencies, and in leadership development, the community has benefited. A year-round women's division is strongly recommended as an instrument to broaden involvement and participation in community work, leadership opportunities, and fundraising achievement. Any skilled executive for the new central organization should know how to integrate women to a greater degree in significant community roles.

6. **Professional Leadership:** There is an emphatic need for stronger professional leadership. Success of the new central organization would depend substantially on the skill of its executive. However, a person with suitable education and experience would not be available at the current very low salary level. A select few of those currently in the community should be provided with training opportunities in the United States, if at all possible. There is indication that Sao Paulo would welcome the idea of a U.S. executive, on a loaned basis selected by the JDC, HIAS, or CJF for this purpose, with a salary subsidized for an initial period to attract a high-quality professional. Lack of knowledge of the Portuguese language would constitute a handicap, which could be made up for in part by a knowledge of Yiddish during an initial period of service. In financial terms, the return on such an investment by the American organizations would be substantial.

7. **Volunteer Leadership:** There should be more emphasis placed on the development of a more skilled and knowledgeable volunteer leadership. This goal could be advanced, in part, through missions of American Jewish leaders to Brazil and training programs for carefully selected leaders within the United States. Such a program could begin with participation by a selected group of Brazilians in the General Assembly of the Council of Jewish Federations, supplemented with planned visits to select U.S. communities. People involved should receive some advance training in order to develop a group spirit. A leadership

program should include ongoing relationships between Brazilian and American community leaders. Curricular material should be carefully selected and provided.

8. **Consultation:** It is probable that in a few years, the Brazilian Jewish community will no longer require financial help. There will be a need, however, for continued advice and direction in community building. There should be a continued presence in the foreseeable future of American professionals, consultants, and advisors. Quick withdrawal of this form of support would constitute a major backward step. It could result in regression for the community concept.

CONCLUSION

The Jewish community of Brazil is following patterns established in the United States generations earlier. Agencies and services that expedite the resettlement and integration of refugees have been aided by American generosity. The community could, however, develop self-sufficiency in the foreseeable future.

Brazil will continue to grow as a cultural mosaic. With a stable government and economy, Jewish people will likely be free to express themselves and share in leadership of the country. It can be anticipated that Jews will be among the leading educators, university professors, artists, scientists, lawyers, and physicians. Jews are also making rapid strides in the business world of Brazil and given economic stability will thrive. Then the Jewish community of Brazil will be able to share responsibility with other Diaspora communities for world Jewish affairs.

REBIRTH: THE EUROPEAN JEWISH COMMUNITY

Presented at the Quarterly Meeting of the Council of Jewish Federations
and Welfare Funds in Washington D.C.
June 1975

Thirty years have elapsed since the end of World War II and the indescribable horror that befell our people. We mourned and then shared in picking up the remnants of survivors and then soon after we gloried in the birth of Israel.

As we looked upon the incomparable catastrophe in Europe, the Jewish people there became as ourselves, for we know that with rare exception it could have been us. There is no separating ourselves from the horror and death. I had myself arrived in America as an infant along with my sister and parents, who were then an ocean away from their many siblings in a large closely knit family, all of whom later perished.

As we reached out in sadness and shared in rescue, relief, and rehabilitation, we asked ourselves whether the Jewish people and Jewish communities could ever again exist in Europe. Would people who had experienced so much travail retain an identity with Judaism and Jewish communities? As we envisioned the map of a new Jewish world we saw Israel as its core—along with America, with small islands of Jews spread throughout the world, and with a continuing diminution of European Jewry. But the Jews of Europe are still with us; out of the ashes they are rebuilding, and their communities are growing and will be renewed.

I no longer have any doubt that they will continue to exist and flourish, but in Jewish communities that will be very different from what they were. For example, the Netherlands Jewish community was reduced from 120,000 to 20,000 people by the end of World War II and now has grown again to 35,000—and it is there to stay. The Dutch community, in contrast to that in pre-war Europe, now has two components, one Orthodox and another liberal, made up of people who are not affiliated with any synagogue but are still actively involved in the community, particularly in times of crisis as with the October 1973 Yom Kippur war.

There are Jewish communities in virtually every country in Europe and in all of the states of the Soviet Union. The movement of Jewish populations from country to country is beginning to end, and we see signs of increasing stability.

I sense a continuing passion among European Jews for their Jewishness. I was in Brussels in September 1972 when the Israeli Olympic athletes were murdered in Munich. I shudder now as I recall the pain of the people, most of whom were Holocaust survivors, as they recoiled in shock. Many of the Belgian Jews, with whom I had grown close, had been Poles or French or Germans or Dutch. Passionate, angry demonstrations the likes of which I had never known took place in Belgium and in all of Europe. Deep feelings of Jewish identity were vehemently expressed.

The ways in which agencies of Jewish life are sustained vary from country to country. In some there is a compulsory tax that Jews, by governmental order, pay to support Jewish institutions. In Sweden such a compulsory tax existed until 1952, when it became voluntary, and most Jews continue to pay it in accordance with a formula based on income. In Switzerland and in some other countries the Jewish community has the right to tax Jewish people for money to sustain domestic agencies, an authority unimaginable in the United States. In addition, all of the countries of Western Europe have fundraising campaigns on behalf of Israel through the Keren Hayesod. The federation idea of unified campaigns is almost unknown, except in France. There the FSJU—Fonds Social Juif Unifie (Unified Jewish Philanthropic Fund)—is moving toward a centralized organization in accordance with the federation idea, in this instance a united campaign conducted in all of France. In most countries and cities, agencies operate independently from each other, and organizations raise money in competition with other organizations.

BUILDING COMMUNITIES

It takes a long time to build a community. The concept is simple, implying common interests and people living and working together in unity. But achievement of the idea is difficult, particularly so for people who have suffered so much because of their identity as Jews. How tempting it is for some to abandon that identity. A question that has been most prevalent among American Jews is whether Jewish communities will survive in freedom. My observations of a blazing rebirth of a Jewish spirit in Europe as well as in America, lead me to answer that question in the affirmative.

Let us consider the situation in France. There are 600,000 Jews in France, twice the 300,000 at the beginning of World War II. By the end of the war only 150,000 Jews lived in France. That number doubled as Jews came from all parts of Europe to France, and then the population was augmented by several hundred thousand newcomers from the Maghreb communities of North Africa—Tunisia, Algeria, and Morocco. More people are coming. The changed community is no longer led by only a few renowned families, such as the Rothschilds. The French-speaking Jews who came from the North African countries now play a major role in community life and share in leadership. There is a slowly emerging integration of the French leadership—Ashkenazic and Sephardic. We can expect that in time there will be a melding of cultures and an increasingly unified approach to community building and problem solving.

In the 1950s during the French-Algerian war, the sympathies of most French people were with the Algerian thrust for independence. I was in France then where I was an eyewitness to the Jewish sympathy for Algeria, which was manifested in demonstrations, mass meetings, and billboards calling for independence. With the recent arrival of large groups of Arab immigrants, many of whom are depressed economically, France is challenged to resettle more people and to maintain reasonable calm among those in want

Today, at the same time as the French government is currying favor with Arab and Muslim countries for oil, trade, and economic gain, the Arab minority within France continues to grow. The doors of France are open to continuing immigration from North African countries, and Moroccan, Tunisian, and Algerian Muslims have been arriving in great numbers.

The French people's displeasure with this growing Arab minority is apparent. Liberal-minded people of France identify with Israel, rather than with the Arab states that confront her in the Middle East. A primary concern of the Jews of France is security, flowing naturally from the history of recent decades. The Jewish people are attentive to relationships with the government, which it is hoped will not be marred by the presence of a large Arab-Muslim population.

It may seem strange to see a Jewish community growing in Germany. Those few who survived there and those who have chosen to return are eager to welcome more Jews into their midst. They want more company in rebuilding a German Jewish community. The German government has been making an impressive effort to encourage an inflow of Jews, facilitating their entry and providing grants to help with resettlement and subsidies for Jewish agencies and institutions. Germany is demonstrating a bias in favor of Jews and enforces strict anti-Nazi laws.

THE 200TH ANNIVERSARY OF THE STOCKHOLM JEWISH COMMUNITY

The European Council of Jewish Communities held its annual meeting in Stockholm in May 1975 to celebrate the 200th anniversary of the founding of the Swedish Jewish community. Leaders of Jewish communities from throughout Europe brought gifts and greetings to this impressive assemblage and were warmly welcomed by the people of Sweden and treated deferentially by public officials. Matters on the agenda included Jewish education, Israel, prejudice and anti-Semitism, and Jewish survival; the program content resembled that of a quarterly or regional conference of our Council of Jewish Federations as they were decades earlier.

There was one uniquely thrilling, uplifting occasion in that celebration of 200 years of Jewish life in Sweden. It took place in a 200-year-old synagogue in the presence of dignitaries, the Prime Minister, the Mayor of Stockholm, other government officials, and leaders of Jewish communities from throughout Europe. Each speaker was introduced by one Jewish leader and, after they spoke, thanked by another Jewish leader for their presence and their words.

The last speaker was Archbishop Olaf Sondby, the head of the church of Sweden. The Archbishop, when introduced, startled the assemblage when he said,

> You have thanked the crown, you have thanked the prime minister, you have thanked the government, me you must not thank—for that what my church has done to your people will forever be an everlasting mark of shame for all of us and I am ashamed. We can never make amends for what we have done but I tell you in the presence of the leaders of the Swedish community and others from throughout Europe that I have on this day issued a directive to all ministers of the church, to all officials, to permit no educational materials to be used in the schools of this country and none are to emanate from the church until reviewed by the rabbinate and the Jewish community so that we can be certain never again of teaching prejudice against Jews.

Indeed, audience members did not applaud, but sat in silent astonishment, seeming numb, and they remained quiet for a considerable time. Afterward the faces of Jews, who had come from so many lands, including people who had survived Holocaust horror, wore smiles and expressions of joy.

The Jewish community of Sweden, which was quite small in 1939, has grown and has absorbed people from many places. The openness of Swedish society provides a great deal of psychological material comfort; for example, it has attracted 8,000 Jews from Poland who have come there to live. The leader of the community, Fritz Hollander, also the president of the European Council of Jewish Community, who emigrated from Germany, is a dynamic businessman comparable to the most influential in the American business world. He is a model of achievement. Chief Rabbi Morton Narrowe, a graduate of the Jewish Theological Seminary in New York, came to Sweden ten years ago when he was quite young, with the expectation that he would serve for a few years, but he is there to stay. People who are not knowledgeable about Judaism may find it difficult to resist assimilation. However, Swedish Jewish leaders believe that the community is not only stronger than it was twenty years ago but that it will be much more so in time to come.

There is pride in Sweden over its involvement in the rescue of 7,000 Danish Jews during World War II and its offer of asylum to 700 Norwegian Jews. In 1956, during the Hungarian uprising, 550 Hungarian Jews escaped to new homes in Sweden.

This remarkable Swedish community has a Jewish community center, built with a grant from the American Jewish Joint Distribution Committee. It is a meeting place and sponsors Israeli folk dancing and Jewish student clubs, and has physical education facilities. Its day school is suitably named Hillel Skolen (Academy)—the same name as in use in Milwaukee and in many communities.

EUROPEAN JEWISH COUNCIL

The Council brings together Jewish people and communities from throughout Europe, much like the Council of Jewish Federations does in North America. A major difference is that most of our communities consist of the people living within a city or metropolitan area, whereas in many parts of Europe a single central federation serves the Jews of an entire country. The European Council brings people of these countries and cities together for mutual examination of subjects of common interest. The International character of the Jewish people, with so many having moved from one country to another, results in mutual understanding.

The still young European Council needs time for growth and nurturing. It does not yet have a well-trained developed cadre of professionals to guide and help develop voluntary leaders. However many of the professionals are committed to their work and constitute a cultured group with a fine potential for further development and achievement. For example, the relatively young new director of the European Council, working in his office in Paris, speaks many languages fluently.

The voluntary leadership includes high-quality people of intellect and skill epitomized by the president of the European Council, Fritz Hollander, who escaped from his native Germany to Sweden. His business has branches throughout Europe, the Americas, and Africa. A sophisticated worldly man, he is strongly devoted to Israel and knows a great deal about Judaism. He and others like him in knowledge and interest represent very suitable partners for the American Jewish community and the people of Israel in worldwide efforts on behalf of Jewish life and in the pursuit of interests of concern to the whole of the Jewish people.

The American Jewish Community, primarily through the Council of Jewish Federations, has had high-level leadership consultations with European communities, leading to a deepened understanding of problems and opportunities for ongoing exchanges. It would be well to have such visits increase and be expanded in content. Doing so would aid in knowledge development within communities and encourage understanding and growth of the federation idea.

I took on the assignment of working with the European Council of Jewish Communities with reservations. I assumed the worst, expecting to find communities weighed down by intractable problems. Instead, I saw communities moving forward. There are of course, substantial differences among people of different countries with dissimilar cultures. One of the greatest disparities is between those who stress the primacy of local institutions and others who press for support for Israel. This issue is easily recognized by American Jewish leaders, for it has been commonplace in our own communal life. Hopefully skilled, diplomatic professionals will be available to help European Jews recognize that building local communities and strengthening Israel can be done simultaneously.

Just as the American Jewish community learned to respect differences between individuals and groups, and to work together out of common interest, so we may we expect such progress in Europe. I believe that such progress will accelerate in the near future and that communities will become stable, stronger, and more creative. Collaboration of American and European Jewish communities will help contribute to the advancement for all Jewish people in the foreseeable future.

There will be continuing need for a JDC presence in Europe for years to come—and hopefully greater opportunities to be helpful should there be additional acceptance of it in Eastern Europe. It is vital that there be attentive emphasis to community organization in future work.

Through the years the Joint Distribution Committee has done great work in helping meet the needs of people and to create necessary agencies and institutions. There will be the need to continue such work for a time to come. It is strongly recommended that in its continuing work, the JDC, augmented by the Council of Jewish Federations and Welfare Funds, emphasize coordination among all services, which should develop in suitable form, country by country, under the guidance of central organizations resembling federations, as in the United States—unifying the people, developing a feeling of community, and making possible carefully thought out, orderly progress in years to come.

BY THE WATERS OF BABYLON

Written at the request of the Milwaukee Jewish Historical Society and adapted
for use in courses on Jewish communities of the world

November 2003

Iraq, a country devastated by dictatorship, war, and conflicts between religious
and ethnic groups, was home to the oldest Diaspora community in the world.
Today in Iraq there are estimated to be only 33 desperately needy Jews
dependent on help from outside Jewish organizations.

But that land, known in ancient times as Sumer and then Mesopotamia, in
which the city of Babylon became dominant, was the birthplace of Abraham,
from which he left for Canaan. It was a land where glorious as well as tragic
chapters in Jewish history transpired.

BABYLONIAN JEWISH COMMUNITY

Settlements of people living an organized communal life existed in that
ancient territory as long ago as 6000 BCE. That land was dominated by as
many peoples and dynasties as any place in the world. Little-known peoples
—the Akkadians, Alamites, Babylonians, Amorites, Hittites, Kassites,
Assyrians, Chaldeans, Parthians, and the Seleucids—were followed by the
Persians under Cyrus the Great who defeated Babylon in battle; later the
Greeks and the Romans occupied the area. Much later other conquerors came
onto the scene—in the 12th century the Seljuks, the Mongols in the 13th, and
later the Mamluks. Taken over by one people after another, the land is now
populated by people who bear no relationship to their ancient predecessors.

The Babylonia and Mesopotamia of antiquity was a place of advanced culture that produced outstanding literature and poetry and surprisingly modern agricultural and public sanitation systems. It was also a seat of impressive Jewish learning. Its great academies of Sura and Pumbedita were looked to for wisdom by Jewish communities everywhere; those academies were succeeded by the Academy of Baghdad, which attracted Jews from various countries.

However, for Jews, Babylonia was often a fearful name. In 586 BCE under King Nebuchadnezzar the Babylonians besieged and burnt Jerusalem, destroyed the Temple, and executed Jewish leaders. Israelites were deported, exiled, and dispersed; large numbers were taken from Judea into slavery in Babylon.

When in 539 BCE Cyrus the Great and his Persians (ancestors of modern-day Iran) conquered Babylon, the Jews were allowed to return to Jerusalem; indeed Cyrus encouraged their return to rebuild the Temple. Some grasped the opportunity, but a majority chose to remain in Babylon. They were loathe to leave the good life they had developed there. Those who returned to Jerusalem, led by Nehemiah and Ezra, were instrumental in re-establishing the Temple in Jerusalem, but those who stayed behind remained strongly attached to their Israel roots as reflected in Psalm 137:

By the waters of Babylon where we sat down
There we sat down yea we wept
When we remember Zion

How shall we sing the Lord's song
In a foreign land?
If I forget thee oh Jerusalem
Let my right hand forget her cunning.

The memories of Jerusalem burning and the Temple in ruins remained vivid in the memory of the exiles, but Cyrus was a just king and Jews expected life under his rule to be comfortable.

Under Persian rule, Babylonia became an extraordinary spiritual center of Jewish life; there the great Babylonian Talmud was compiled. Jewish life flourished, and great academies prospered until the 11th century CE when

Islam became the predominant religion of the region. Jewish life in ancient Babylon through the first twelve centuries of the Common era was organized on an egalitarian basis, much like the Kehillah of European society. The community was headed by an exilarch* elected by the Jewish people themselves and approved by Muslim authority. Substantial power was vested in the exilarch, and the people were required to obey him. He dispensed justice, which could include fines, imprisonment, or flogging. He was responsible for supervising charitable funds and collecting taxes from the Jews.

UNDER THE RULE OF ISLAM

For hundreds of years Jewish life ebbed and flowed, dependent substantially on the ruler of the land at any given time. As Islam spread and took over the land, Jews were "tolerated" under demeaning conditions. There were many times of stress and persecution for Jews. Lives were lost in frequent pogroms and synagogues were desecrated. Persecution by Muslim mobs was always a threat; such mob violence continued until the 19th century.

Under the rule of Islam, Jews and Christians were regarded as Dhimmis (protected people). The conditions of life for them were spelled out eventually in the Covenant of Omar, which required that Dhimmis pay special taxes and pledge not to insult Islam, attempt to convert Muslims to other religions, betray the government to its enemies, or build new churches or synagogues.

The regulations obliged the government to "protect" the lives and property of non-Muslims, whose freedom was guaranteed with certain restrictions. Legally, Jews as well as Christians were regarded as second-class citizens; their testimony was generally not accepted in a Muslim court. They were expected to hold positions inferior to the Muslims and generally were treated with scorn, unless they succumbed to the pressure to convert to Islam. At times they were required to wear special distinctive yellow clothes. They were prohibited from wearing swords or riding horses; even when riding donkeys

---

* *First reference to Exilarch is in reference to leaders of the Jews of the Babylonian exile. The Exilarch was a person of high standing, at the times of Davidic origin, i.e., regarded as a descendant of the house of David. In Arabic times the Exilarch had special status in Muslim circles, access to rulers, and involvement in political aspects of governance.*

they were required to dismount upon meeting a Muslim. Jews, like Christians, were confined to special quarters that were usually shut up after dark and were not permitted to enter certain parts of Muslim cities.

Despite all the discrimination, the situation of Jews in the Muslim world in the Middle Ages was not quite as bad as in the Christian world where they were often accused of being "Christ killers."

THE SYKES-PICOT PACT

The country now known as Iraq did not exist until relatively modern times. Its origins lay in World War I, stemming from the Sykes-Picot Pact negotiated in secret in 1916 by mid-level diplomats, Sir Mark Sykes of Britain and Francois Georges Picot of France. That agreement, in the midst of World War I, charted out plans for the disposition and future of lands of the Ottoman Empire, which was to be dismembered. The French, and particularly the British, sought the cooperation of influential Arabs in this effort and made promises to them. They dealt primarily with the two most powerful families on the Arabian Peninsula—the Sa'uadis and the Husayn—which had deep mutual hostility toward each other, expressed in frequent warfare.

Leading the negotiations were the heads of the families. Husayn Ibn Ali, who had been keeper of the holiest place in Islam, Mecca, represented the Sultan of the Ottoman Empire on behalf of the Husayn family. He had the unique honor of being a Shareef, or noble, for to be a Shareef was to be a descendant of Mohammed himself. He referred to his family as the Hashemites.

The second family, the Sa'uadis, was headed by Abdul Aziz Ibn Saud, lord of the Nejd, a vice royalty in the area in which the city of Riyadh, the capital of Saudi Arabia now stands.

As rewards for these families' cooperation, three kingdoms were eventually established, Saudi Arabia for the Sa'uadi family and for the Husayn family Transjordan and Iraq; three countries carved out of land held by the Ottoman Empire. Husayn Ibn Ali's favorite son Abdullah was to become king of Transjordan, and another son, Feisal, made famous by his friendship with T.E. Lawrence (Lawrence of Arabia), was eventually installed as king of the newly created country, Iraq.

Just as the secret Sykes-Picot agreement provided for division of much of the Arabic-speaking Middle East, other secret agreements provided for Russia and Italy to annex portions of what is now Turkey. President Woodrow Wilson, suspecting that allied governments were involved in secret agreements with one another to aggrandize their empires, feared that such developments would confirm the charges that he was involving the United States in a war that served essentially imperialistic interests. Upon Wilson's demand, the British Foreign Secretary, Arthur Balfour, sent copies of the agreements to Washington. Wilson's political confidant, Edward Mandell House (known as Colonial House), who remarked upon seeing them, "They are making it a breeding place for future war."

Wilson, then fighting as an ally of Britain and France, was in the anomalous situation of joining them in war against Germany and Austro-Hungary without being at war with the Ottoman Empire. Wilson believed that the need to keep the agreements secret impugned his integrity. Subsequently, Wilson in his then-famous "Fourteen Points" outline, demanded that there be no more secret agreements between countries and that diplomacy and negotiations should always take place in public view.

THE BRITISH MANDATE AND THE EARLY YEARS OF STATEHOOD

Subsequent to the war, the newly organized League of Nations presented to Britain a "mandate." Under the British Mandate, Britain would be responsible for the administration of territories that had been Palestine and Mesopotamia, land out of which Transjordan, Iraq, and much later Israel was to be carved. Iraq became a state formally in 1932 with Feisal of the Husayn family as king.

During the Mandate period, and in the early days of Iraq as a state, the Jews enjoyed freedom of religion, felt little discrimination in employment, and were able to create their own education system. They were elected to the Iraqi Parliament and participated freely in all government institutions. Ezekiel Sassoon, a member of the famous Sassoon family sometimes referred to as the Rothschilds of the East, was Minister of Finance from 1920-1923. This extraordinary Jewish family can be traced to David Sassoon, born in 1792 into a Sephardic Jewish family in Baghdad. Not unlike the Rothschilds, Sassoon sons and relatives migrated to other lands, setting up branches of the Sassoon company in India and China, most prominently in Shanghai.

Well educated and often fluent in Arabic, Hebrew, English, and French, Jews in Iraq rose to positions of dominance. Jewish firms controlled 70 percent of the import trade and 40 percent of the exports. There were many Jewish authors of note in Iraq who wrote in Arabic and who translated into Arabic literature from other languages.

As in earlier times, the Jewish community was organized in a Kehillah style, in which an informal government of the Jews themselves operated their own affairs, financed by funds contributed by members of the community. Hebrew education was treated as a basic communal responsibility; teachers were brought in from Palestine. Zionism was a dominant element of Jewish life in Iraq. The Zionist society of Mesopotamia with Aaron Sassoon as its president was founded in 1921.

The 19,000 Kurdish Jews living in Northern Iraq did not share the prosperous experience of other Jews. The Kurdish population was poor; illiteracy was widespread among the Jews as well as the general Kurdish population. There were few educational institutions and women remained completely illiterate. However, the relationship between Jews and the Kurdish Muslims was good and after the State of Israel was created in 1948, it was even better. The Kurds, themselves victims of oppression, sympathized with the Jews; larger Kurdish tribes guarded Jews, keeping them safe from robbery and murder. However, by 1951 there were no Jews left in the Kurdish portion of Iraq, Israel having become their home.

The good times in Iraq did not last very long after expiration of the Mandate and Iraq independence. Nazi propaganda spread through the country; hostilities reached a climax in riots on Shavuot in 1941 when hundreds of Jews were tortured and murdered with full government knowledge and with no intercession. Synagogues were destroyed and property was looted. The situation improved when the British entered to save the situation early in World War II.

In 1942 the "Babylonia Pioneer Movement" was created. It taught the Hebrew language and Zionist ideology. Programs of immigration from Iraq to then Palestine were organized both legally and illegally; young people were taught the use of firearms for self-defense.

On May 4, 1948 with the proclamation of the State of Israel, martial law was declared in Iraq and Jews were forbidden to emigrate. With martial law came military courts. An earlier law that punished those found guilty of being Communists with a minimum of seven years of imprisonment up to a sentence of death was amended to include Zionism as well. The accusation of Zionism was easy to make and to prove; it required only the testimony of two witnesses and there was no appeal of sentences. Several Jews were hanged for the offense of Zionism. The objective of the government was twofold: to halt the underground Jewish immigration movement and to enrich the government with the money of Jews, who were forced to pay heavy fines or who escaped the country, leaving their property behind. As late as 1969, eleven prominent Jewish businessmen were hanged in a Baghdad public square. Thousands of onlookers cheered the sight.

Iraq became a full participant in hostilities against Israel in 1948 at Israel's birth and in the 1967 Six-Day War. In 1956, Israel along with France and Britain took military action against Egypt and its president, Gamal Abdel Nasser, who had closed the Suez Canal. Iraq sent troops into Jordan to join the fight on Egypt's side and the exodus of Jews from Iraq increased.

In 1950 Iraq permitted Jews to emigrate, provided they would relinquish their Iraqi nationality. A mass exodus entitled "Operation Ezra" took place, which was followed by "Operation Nehemiah." Helped by an underground organization led by Israelis, 23,500 Iraqi-born Jews escaped Iraq and settled in Israel. Jews who left legally could take with them $140.00 per adult and $60.00 per child. All other assets—approximately $200 million dollars—were sequestered by Iraq.

A TINY REMNANT

Active Jewish life in Iraq has come to an end. Of the 140,000 Jews who lived in Iraq in 1939, many experiencing the good life, there now remains a remnant of 33 known Jews. Among them are a 90-year-old man with no family who lived in a Jewish community shelter for 19 years and a frail 86- year-old man who lives in a synagogue. An elderly woman without family, who broke her back six years ago and for whom no surgery has been available, survives in constant pain.

A long history of Judaism in Iraq is ending, leaving behind glorious chapters. Yet, remnants of the Jews of antiquity in Babylon remain evident today. In ancient Nineveh, the city that is now Mosul, there is a gravesite that Islamic tradition holds to be the grave of Jonah. Iraqis describe a mosque there as having been a synagogue in ancient times. American soldiers now in Iraq have been discovering old synagogues and some Yeshivot.

It is difficult to imagine the existence of a Jewish community in Iraq ever again.

ISRAEL AND THE DIASPORA: ONE PEOPLE

Keynote address to the Seminar for Executives given at a meeting of the Council of Jewish Federations in Hilton Head, SC.

July 1983

ONE PEOPLE

We Jews are one people, irrespective of where we live, and the existence of Israel is central to the future and destinies of every Jew. Israel's existence and conduct have renewed Jewish pride; given the world Jewish community a sense of social dynamism, intellectual progress, and cultural power; and made it possible for hundreds and thousands of our people to go from the depths of despair to a new life and new hope.

Clearly, Jews in Israel and Jews in the Diaspora need each other. Yet in everyday life, the relationship is complicated by some differences in orientation and in our reactions to issues.

Let me define terms for this discussion. Diaspora is used in the context of a voluntary dispersion of the Jewish people, which is different from *galut*, a people uprooted from a homeland and exiled. Jews were in *galut* from the time of the destruction of the Second Temple in 70 CE to the creation of the State of Israel in 1948. Today, most Jews can choose to live in Israel. Most Americans do not make that choice; we live in the Diaspora, feeling closely connected to Israel. Conditions are different in some other countries, such as the Soviet Union and her neighboring communist countries and Iran, but that does not constitute exile in the ordinary sense.

Having lived in the Diaspora for hundreds of years, we have taken on the colorings of the lands in which we live. In most Jewish communities, Jews have organized their own institutions, established autonomous systems of education, practiced Judaism, and, most important, developed methods of organization for self-perpetuation.

Establishment of Jewish communities around the world is an extraordinary historical odyssey. If it were not for certain unique events, some of them pure accident, the American Jewish community might never have developed to today's size and importance. After all, much of the movement of Jews to the United States came from Russia after the assassination of Czar Alexander II in 1881, under whose fairly liberal regime the lot of Jews improved, as opportunities never before available in education, business, professions, and employment opened. But with Alexander II's assassination, his second son, Czar Alexander III, set Russia on a brutal reactionary course with Jews as its chief victims. There were pogroms and passage of legislation restricting Jewish mobility and access to work and education. A trickle of Jewish migration to the United States became a flood.

From 1881 to World War I, two million Jews left Eastern Europe for America, first younger people, the poor, and the uneducated, to be followed by the older, more educated, and more skilled. Jews from all ends of the religious spectrum came, from the religiously observant who established synagogues immediately on arrival to secular or non-religious revolutionaries, all bound together by a common past and hope for a better life. Yiddish-speaking greenhorns became Americanized, moved into the working class, and attained white-collar status—moving from peddlers to merchants, from pants pressers to clothing manufacturers. We survived periods of overt anti-Semitism; discrimination in employment, housing, and college admissions; and the horror of Nazism over the entire world. America was hospitable to the development of our cultural forms, and discrimination against Jews began to diminish. Jews became part and parcel of America. There have even been times when it has been "in" to be Jewish.

Then came the 1960s and the Six-Day War, which elevated Jewish pride and dedication to Israel. The 1973 Yom Kippur War was followed by the 1975 United Nations "Zionism is racism" resolution and the resultant manifestations of anti-Semitism. But we survived and we developed a greater sense of self-acceptance.

After an initial negative reaction toward the Diaspora, most Israelis felt a growing acceptance of it, particularly of the American Jewish community. They recognize that most American Jews cannot or will not migrate, even as they remain unwavering in support of Israel.

COMPONENTS OF THE ISRAEL-DIASPORA RELATIONSHIP
Political Support

The Jackson-Vanik Amendment is the direct result of political influence of American Jews expressed in consort with the leaders of Israel. Linking trade policy to the emigration policies of Communist bloc countries, it also reflects the value of an American Jewish Diaspora. This year, President Reagan notified Congress that he would extend most favored nation trade status to Romania following assurances from the Romanian president that the education tax on Romanian emigrants would be dropped. That education tax, $10,000 per head, had been in effect since November 1982 in clear violation of the Jackson-Vanik Amendment.

This example of American Jewish political power is in sharp contrast to our situation in the 1920s and 30s when the American Jewish community hardly counted politically. We were then still largely a first- and second-generation immigrant population with relatively few Jews of wealth or power. We were so busy assimilating and trying to be like other people and were powerless to confront Hitlerism. Power results from ways in which a group can and makes itself heard. We had little influence, did not organize well, and so were never a united force on behalf of the Jews of Europe.

Since World War II, Jews have risen on the economic ladder at an accelerated pace and we've learned the importance of political involvement. We are no longer fearful and powerless. Now, we create political action committees, have an effect on issues important to us and support candidates with positive attitudes toward Israel. We developed the American-Israel Public Affairs Committee. Many Jews, who had little to do with political processes, entered into them out of concern for Israel. Support for Israel became a primary concern of American Jewry.

As a community, we have three strengths that enhance our political power:

1. We vote in a higher proportion than any other identifiable group in the United States—as high as 92% of us voted in the last three federal elections. That amounts to real voting power, especially in certain states.

2. We give time and energy and money to political candidates who understand our concerns.

3. We are concerned with a variety of issues that span the political spectrum, but take a leading role on those that concern Israel. We are joined in that support by organized labor and a growing portion of the evangelical Christian community for reasons of its own.

Human Resources

In contrast to the political arena in which we provide clearly visible support for Israel, Israelis find us deficient in an area of great need—reinforcement of manpower.

Israel needs more people—a population of 3.5 million is not large enough to keep Israel secure from threats made by hostile, confrontational states and to safeguard its culture. The modest rate of immigration into Israel, particularly from Western countries, the outflow of Sabras and Western-oriented Israelis, and the high birth rates of Sephardic Jews are changing the makeup of Israeli society from Western toward Middle Eastern. The character of the nation is affected by the possession of the West Bank and Gaza, as well as the growing numbers of the Arab population in Israel proper. There are fears that, should Israel absorb the West Bank, it would alter its Jewish character, a key argument against permanent retention of that territory, an opinion with which an estimated one-half of the Israeli population agrees.

An Israel with its current 3.5 million Israelis is vastly different than one with 5 million, the number most Israelis feel the country should now have. The lack of Aliyah from the United States leads to reservations by Israelis in considering our views.

As Abba Eban puts it, "You are caught up in that deadly gap between the ardor of your rhetoric and the totally inadequate nature of your involvement."

Eban is saying that we are willing to give a bit of our money and advice, but not our bodies, our souls, or our children. Zevulon Hammer, the education minister, tells us, "We appreciate your economic and political support; however, what we really need is the dream of your Jewish soul."

Aliyah has simply not been a major feature of American Jewish life. Only 3,000 people, of whom 2,000 were over age 65, moved from the United States and Canada to Israel in 1982. Although Aliyah was stimulated recently in part by the economic recession in the United States, the upswing is temporary. Israeli Shlichim in our communities offer advice as an aid with Aliyah; they do not overtly press it, knowing of the resistance of many parents and family members to separation from their sons and daughters.

Religion—A Divisive Issue

One issue that drives us apart is religion. We in America live in a religiously pluralistic society. Although the state of Israel was the creation primarily of a secularized Jewry, secularized Jews are in conflict with ultra religious Israelis, who press to amend the Law of Return and the definition of "Who is a Jew," which would limit the ability of converts to become Israeli citizens, keeping citizenship open only to those converted under Orthodox Jewish auspices.

At the last General Assembly of the Council of Jewish Federations in November 1982, a committee on religious issues in Israel judged it would be inappropriate for the CJF to deal with religious issues, lacking consensus within Jewish federations and people in North America on the issue. However, it did find widespread concern over the possibility of change in the Law of Return and general agreement that such action could have a divisive impact in North American communities and on the relationships between Israel and North American Jewry. Passage of a "Who is a Jew" bill invalidating conversions by non-Orthodox rabbis by inserting the words "according to Halacha" into the law could diminish Aliyah.

Other Barriers to a Close Relationship

The American Jewish community is a voluntary grouping. The Israeli government represents a sovereign state. There are worlds of difference in the ways in which we talk to each other, and some of them showed up in some

American Jewish reactions to the Lebanese War. The State of Israel was founded by dreamers and idealists. The German sociologist Max Weber's* concept of an ethics of ideology compared to the ethics of pragmatism and responsibility is relevant in this context. Inevitably, however, the pragmatic facts of life of creating and running a sovereign state have had great moderating effects on the Zionist dreams of Israel's founders.

For 1,900 years, the Jewish people were powerless and stateless. We indulged in and postulated idealistic views on what our behavior would be in a state of our own. We could not test these theories in practice. Everything changed in 1948 when Israel became a state. The Israelis needed time to adjust to their changed role. In early years of statehood, Israel pursued some of the ethics and ideals of pre-state theory, still common among Jews in the Diaspora. It refused to establish diplomatic relations with Spain—a fascist regime. It accepted reparations from Germany, but not diplomatic relations.

Israel's relationship with South Africa illustrated a compromise between Jewish ideals and pragmatic realities. The guiding ideology of Israel, in a strong belief in equality and a brotherhood of humanity, is opposite to the philosophy of the state of South Africa, based on apartheid—the presumed supremacy of one race over another. Guided by ideology alone, Israel would eschew relations with South Africa, thus obtaining favor with many Third World nations. But the Jewish State must consider the effect of such action on the South African Jewish community; thus Israel mutes its opposition to apartheid, exposing itself to criticism for maintaining relations. It acts in a way that sovereign states usually react.

Another seeming conflict exists in the Jewish traditional emphasis on peace and Israel's status as one of the largest arms merchants in the world. Yet, to protect itself with an up-to-date weapons arsenal, Israel must produce arms and it must have a market for its overproduction. That is not militarism—it is self-preservation.

Here now is a Jewish state—the only one and it relates to other states in many of which there are Jewish communities. These considerations affect its

---

* Max Weber, (1864-1920) one of the founders of modern study of sociology and public administration.

foreign policy. It needs to ask itself constantly what impact its decisions will make on the Jewish world. How does it create suitable relationships with Argentina—yet serving the best interests of 450,000 Jews there? How does it help the Jewish people of Brazil living under a military dictatorship?

If we unreservedly support Israel's domestic and foreign policy, then we are accused of reacting in a knee-jerk way. If we are critical, then we are accused of creating an atmosphere that could result in diminished support by the United States.

To ask world Jewry to maintain silence on issues in Israel is to relegate the Diaspora to a secondary position; it is in effect to say that Jewish support should be material and political but should not contain intellectual dimensions. If we pursue our relationships in accordance with such limitations, then the Jewish world would have reduced involvement with Israel. Moreover, events in Israel affect American-Jewish interests. World Jewry has a substantial role in interpreting Israel to the world. It would be unwise for us to be omitted from discussions on policies we are called upon to explain. Diaspora Jewry must have access to active dialogue with Israel about policies. A real problem would come not from substantial involvement of the Diaspora, but on the contrary, from Jewish apathy and detachment. The question is not whether we should express ourselves, but rather how we do so constructively.

Israelis themselves want to hear our opinions. For example, Golda Meir, after the Yom Kippur War said, "We want to hear nice things about ourselves, but we must also hear the truth. Anti-Semites criticism we ignore. American Jews are Mishpacha; they are our family and from them we expect not only praise, but criticism as well." Joseph Berg, a key political figure and Cabinet minister, had this to say: "There has to be a capacity on our part to comment on the affairs of Israel, since all Jews are one."

Zevulon Hammer, the Minister of Education, said to us last November, "Share with us in a spirit of empathy in the building of the state. Share with us the burden uniting nationalism with love and justice. Speak critically from personal concern, from serious involvement. You are not outsiders and strangers who have no stake in the quality of life in Israel. Judaism is your future. It is not enough to write a check for the UJA, buy Bonds, or send support for our security needs."

The period immediately after the 1982 Lebanon War was the most difficult period in American-Israeli relationships since the Sinai Campaign in 1956. The pain of the war was great. For the first time, Israel had initiated a war when, in the view of many, it was not under immediate attack. Many Arab civilians suffered when PLO terrorists living among them were attacked. Deliberate atrocities were committed by Arab Christians on Arab Muslims in an area under Israeli military control.

Just as Israel has to strike a balance between its ideals and pragmatic reality, it has to balance the need to be popular and the need to survive. In waging the Lebanese war, Israel chose to retain life. Alive, Israel can work to reconstruct its popularity. If dead, Israel might be a very popular corpse during the funeral oration, meaningless consolation.

In the wake of the war in Lebanon, some Jewish groups expressed themselves in public without restraint. Some were limited in their ardor for Israel when it behaved in ways that did not please them. Some members of Congress and the political administration solicited Jewish criticism of Israel. Some Jewish fair-weather friends criticized Israel just to show what good Americans they were.

American Jews should exercise care and caution regarding public criticism of Israel on security issues. Lacking experience of life under continuous stress and frequent warfare, we often view Israel as having an obsession with security. Israel may welcome our advice but only Israel can make decisions about its security. If anything goes wrong, the sacrifice of life will be borne by Israelis alone. If we want to have a role in decisions of war and peace, then we have an obligation to serve in the Israeli military or have our children do so, sharing the danger. As the great Athenian warrior-statesman, Pericles (ca. 450 BCE), shouted to his troops, "If you will not endure the battle, then you must not covet to the spoils."

Just as Israeli public officials should refrain from interceding in American elections, American Jewish leaders should stay clear of interference with

Israeli political elections. I recall that in 1976 when Menachem Begin, in the midst of a campaign to be prime minister, spoke at the Jewish Community Center in Milwaukee; people made contributions to his campaign. This could be regarded as interference by Americans in an Israeli political election.

Israeli public officials should express themselves on American government positions as they affect Israel. It is proper for them to argue the merits of a united Jerusalem and to express disappointment with the American government's position, but it would be indiscreet for them to publicly urge American Jews to petition their Congressmen or to descend on the White House. American Jewry itself is now sensitive enough to initiate action.

Israel needs American Jews to participate in a constructive dialogue on four issues:

1. Political strategy—how to deal with foes, friends, and potential friends.

2. Israel's economy—how to exploit its greatest resource—manpower—and how American Jewry can help in this effort.

3. Nation building—fostering a unified society through such programs as Project Renewal.

4. Aliyah—the need to increase Israel's population through immigration from the West.

Philanthropy

Our direct philanthropic links to Israel have been through the United Jewish Appeal, the United Israel Appeal, and primarily through the Jewish Agency for Israel.

The United Jewish Appeal is our channel for aid. It is a service instrument for federations—no more, no less. The United Israel Appeal is a major beneficiary. But the Jewish Agency is our real partner, and yet we have oftentimes had only an amorphous relationship with it.

The Jewish Agency had its foundations in the First World Zionist Congress initiated by Theodore Herzl in 1897; in the Balfour Declaration calling for the creation of a Jewish national home in 1917; and in the British Mandate of 1922 giving the British the responsibility for governance of Palestine and providing for the formation of a Jewish agency to represent the Jewish population in Palestine.

The Jewish Agency is our largest beneficiary agency. From the time of its creation in 1929 by Chaim Weitzman, then president of the World Zionist Organization (WZO), until statehood was achieved in 1948, it served as the informal government of the Jews in Palestine. As an instrument of the WZO, it received the lion's share of campaign funds raised by the American Jewish community channeled through the United Jewish Appeal. People who ran it were part of the fabric of the Zionist movement. After statehood, some leaders questioned the true worth of the WZO. Prime Minister David Ben Gurion said of the Zionist movement, "We have built a state; we no longer need the scaffolding." The WZO was the scaffold.

The Jewish Agency is an organization with two partners: (1) Zionists organizations through the WZO and (2) world Jewish communities, often referred to by the Zionist partner as fundraisers. In an effort to bring the two groups together, the "Jerusalem program" was adopted in 1968. The Zionists were surprised then by the "fundraisers'" alacrity in acceptance of their principles set out as follows:

1. Unity of the Jewish people and the centrality of Israel in Jewish life.

2. Ingathering of the Jewish people in its historic homeland, Eretz Yisrael, through Aliyah from all countries.

3. Strengthening of the state of Israel based on the prophetic vision of justice and peace.

4. Preservation of the identity of the Jewish people through a fostering of Jewish and Hebrew education and Jewish spiritual and cultural values.

5. Protection of Jewish rights everywhere.

In 1971, the newly reconstituted Jewish Agency provided for equal sharing in its governance between the WZO and the Jewish communities of the world; the Jewish Agency remained, however, to a considerable degree an instrument of the WZO.

The annual assembly of the Jewish Agency was held recently in Jerusalem. Of its 340 delegates, 170 are representatives of the WZO, and 170 of Jewish communities of the world. Its 62-member board of governors is divided in the same way. Its 13-member executive, including the chairs of the major departments—immigration, aliyah, and rural resettlement—carries on its day-to-day work. The 170 seats of the WZO are apportioned to Zionist organizations in accordance with the number of votes received by related political parties in the last election in Israel. The WZO also picks the department chairs, subject to acquiescence of the leaders of the Jewish Agency.

In its recent meeting, the delegates voted down the WZO's appointment of a department chair for the department of Aliyah, the first time the right to dissent was exercised. When, in response, the WZO suggested a shift, a trade-off in chairs, community representatives, insisting on full equality, stood firm and did not go along.

There remains a substantial job to be done in strengthening the partnership so that those who represent the communities share equally with Zionist elements in decision-making. As it stands today, we have reason for some real questioning about this partnership. Of the Jewish Agency's budget of $360 million for 1983-84, $242 million comes from the U.S. Jewish communities through the United Israel Appeal and $23 million from the Keren Hayesod in other countries. Keren Hayesod contributions from other countries are not restricted to non-political charitable work. Thus, in addition to the money raised for the Jewish Agency budget, Keren Hayesod allocates $37 million to the WZO, which together with another $15 million government allocation can be used as the WZO pleases. That means it can be used for programs beyond the Green Line or even for Jewish education in America. This process leaves open the possibility that new services can be created even within American communities whether we deem them worthy or not. There have been instances of such developments within American communities, financed by the WZO, in communities, which had themselves previously considered such projects and determined them to be contrary to the community's interests, needs, or well-being. Such intrusion by one partner, the WZO, in the affairs of the other partner, a community, is illogical and undesirable. It is seen by responsible community leaders as interference, exacerbated by the use of community raised funds.

Person-to-Person Connections

In recent years, there has been an increasing emphasis on missions to Israel. They serve as an introduction for Americans, enhancing relationships. Missions are of course, a beginning, not an end. Hopefully, they will expand and be increased.

Project Renewal has been taking these person-to-person connections to a much deeper level by establishing direct relations between communities of the Diaspora and communities in Israel. It has provided a sense of involvement that enables the federation campaign to offset undesirable competition from individual fundraising campaigns run by Israel-based organizations, which are sometimes distracting from our central efforts to help Israel. Campaigns by some Jewish based organizations offer to donors a sense of personal involvement and recognition that could not be offered by our federation. Such personal involvement can now be provided and encouraged through Project Renewal.

Project Renewal means an opportunity for more genuine understanding of the problems of the disadvantaged in Israeli society. It offers the opportunity to learn about Sephardic cultures and to discover that Sephardi Jews are not foreign to us. Through cultural exchanges, Israelis can learn about American Jews and the American Jewish community, of which they know very little.

Project Renewal enhances the partnership between the Diaspora and the people of Israel. It has had an unexpected side effect. Some people, frustrated with the bureaucracy, both within the Jewish Agency and American establishments have now developed helpful, direct relationships with their twin communities in Israel.

STRENGTHENING THE ISRAEL-DIASPORA RELATIONSHIP

There are many ways we can strengthen the Israel-Diaspora relationship. We need to depoliticize the United Jewish Appeal and the Jewish Agency for Israel. We need to reach out to the growing number of people we call Yordim, Israelis who have settled on our shores. We need to see to it that the Jewish Agency and WZO money is used in our communities only with our consent. We need to recognize that many things precious within Israel flow from what we have done; and that AIPAC, business investment, and Israel Bonds are all creations by people who received their basic training within our communities and within the United Jewish Appeal. We also need to understand that Aliyah will succeed only if we support it.

There is little knowledge in Israel of American Jewry. Israel media in the United States are primarily in Washington D.C., reporting on the American political scene. There is little reporting or knowledge of American Jewish communities. Israelis who visit us are startled when they see a vibrant Jewish life. Relationships would be served by added Israeli exploration and knowledge of American Jewish communities.

We need well-developed instruments for communication. NCRAC, AIPAC, and the Presidents' Conference all play an important role, but it is time for the community to place the Israel-Diaspora relationship on its front burner. The central party to dialogue must be the central instrument of the American Jewish community, our federations. A new era of communications on Israel-Diaspora relations needs to be developed by the federations and they must be equal to the task.

THE CATHOLIC CHURCH AND THE JEWISH PEOPLE: RECONCILIATION AND RAPPROCHEMENT, A REVOLUTIONARY HISTORIC CORRECTION

Digest of a monograph
used in teaching courses—Jewish Communities of the World
May 2000

On March 12, 2000, the first Sunday of Lent, a period of penitence, Pope John Paul II made an unprecedented request for pardon. The public act of repentance, woven into the liturgy of Sunday Mass inside St. Peter's Basilica, included a request for forgiveness by Jews for acts by the Catholic Church committed for more than 2,000 years, with specific reference to the Crusades and the Inquisition. A week later in Israel, the head of the largest Christian denomination in the world expressed grief over the Holocaust and said, "I know how we failed to hear their cry—no words are strong enough to deplore the terrible memory of the Shoah." Condemning anti-Semitism, he reiterated the cry, "Never again," and called for a new relationship between Christians and Jews.

Some people welcomed the Pope's statement as an honorable act, a readiness to admit errors in the past, and a major step toward the diminution of anti-Semitism. Others have expressed disappointment because they had hoped for more; that is, an apology for the silence of the Church and the inaction of Pope Pius XII during the Holocaust.

However, any informed observer who is aware that the Pope, who had had close Jewish friends in his childhood in Poland, is the first pontiff to pray in the Grand Synagogue of Rome and who had established full diplomatic relations between the Vatican and the state of Israel in the face of internal Church opposition, appreciates the significance of the Pope's acts and statements. What has occurred has unique significance in that it comes in the first year of a new millennium and a jubilee year, a time when, as the Pope said on March 12, "The Church kneels before God and implores forgiveness for the present and past sins of its sons."

The time now is most spiritually sacred in Catholic terms. A year of holy jubilee, which takes place every 25 years, is a period of atonement for individuals and for the Church when it itself seeks redemption from sin or mistakes. The jubilee year is regarded as God's year of grace, a time in which Christians earn special indulgences to help secure a place in heaven.

In November, 1999, at a 25th anniversary event of the Catholic-Jewish conference in Milwaukee, Archbishop Rembert Weakland expressed the view that centuries of anti-Semitic Catholic teaching had helped make the Holocaust possible. "By preaching the doctrine that the Jewish people were unfaithful, hypocritical and God-killers, [Catholics] reduced the human dignity of our Jewish brothers and sisters and created attitudes that made reprisals against them seem like acts of conformity to God's will." The people present, including religious leaders and scholars, both Catholic and Jewish, were stunned by the Archbishop's words when he asked forgiveness "for all the teaching and preaching in Catholic churches that may have led up to the Holocaust."

Archbishop Weakland's statement inspired words from other Church leaders. Bishop Daniel A. Hart of Norwich, Connecticut, in a meeting of Jews and Catholics on Ash Wednesday, described the jubilee year as a time of sadness and also a time of reconciliation and celebration leading to renewal and freedom from sin. The jubilee image, he said, had been taught to Christians by "our elder brothers and sisters in faith, the Jewish people." He issued a challenge as Archbishop Weakland had done, for "a new future in which there would be no more anti-Judaism among Christians."

The Bishop of the Greater Milwaukee Synod of the Evangelical Lutheran Church of America, Peter Rogness, in a statement said that Archbishop Weakland's words "reflect the sentiment shared by many in the wider Christian community—including myself. It is my hope . . . there is broad commitment throughout the Christian community that hatred and discrimination have no place here."

At the time of the Jewish High Holy days last fall, Cardinal John O'Connor of New York wrote a letter to the Jewish people reflecting upon pain inflicted on Jews. He wrote, "I ask this Yom Kippur that you understand my own abject sorrow for any member of the Catholic Church, high or low, including myself, who may have harmed you or your forebears in any way." This letter was reprinted as a full-page ad in the *New York Times*. Elie Wiesel, Nobel Prize winner, commented, "For the Prince of the Church to say the things he does, it's very strong. He went far and it's a great gesture of understanding."

The Archbishop of Denver, Charles J. Chaput, in a letter to Jewish people at the end of Hanukkah, wrote, "The Christian faith is rooted in the Jewish people. In persecuting God's chosen people down through the centuries, in ignoring or cooperating in violence against Jews during this century, too many Christians, including Catholics and most shamefully even some ordained to do God's ministry within the Church, have betrayed the gospel. On behalf of Catholics throughout the archdiocese of Denver and for myself alone I ask your forgiveness for the wrongs committed by Catholics against the Jewish people in the past . . . I ask your help in beginning again as brothers and sisters."

The French Bishop's Conference led by Cardinal Jean-Marie Lustiger, in 1997 issued a document entitled "The Declaration of Repentance" in which the Catholic Church of France took responsibility for "failing to lend its aid" to the Jews being persecuted by Nazis—"we beg God's pardon and we call upon the Jewish people to hear our words of repentance." Cardinal Lustiger had been born Jewish in Poland; his mother, who died in Auschwitz, saved her young son's life by concealing his Jewishness, having him baptized and placing him into a Catholic school in Poland. He became a priest and eventually a Cardinal, the most influential churchman in France. Yet Lustiger regards himself still to be a Jew and has stated, "To say that I am no longer a Jew is like denying my father and mother, my grandfathers and grandmothers. I am as Jewish as all other members of my family who were butchered in Auschwitz or in other camps."

CHURCH OF SWEDEN

Prior to the statement by Archbishop Weakland, the most electrifying statement I had ever read came from the head of the Church of Sweden in May 1975. In commemoration of the 200th anniversary of the founding of an organized Jewish community in Sweden, the European Council of Jewish Communities, an association of all Jewish communities in Europe, held its annual meeting in Stockholm, Sweden. As advisor for the Jewish communities of Europe, I, along with European leaders, in the presence of King Gustaf the XVI and principals of political and religious life in Sweden, was startled by the words of Archbishop Olaf Sondby, head of the Church of Sweden following words of welcome to Swedish political leaders. He said, "You have thanked the crown, you have thanked the prime minister, me you must not thank, for that which my church has done to your people for two thousand years will forever be a mark of shame and I am ashamed." The Archbishop announced issuance of a directive to the clergy and leaders of the school system that no book or printed matter was to be used in the schools or churches of Sweden without review by the Jewish community to ensure that the material was not prejudicial. The Jewish leaders present, from many countries in Europe, who had experienced persecution, torture, and the death of loved ones, and had fought for their lives and were then fighting for continuity for the Jewish people, were stunned by the words of the Archbishop that enriched their souls.

In addition to Church leaders, heads of state and community leaders have expressed feelings in the same general spirit. In 1994, Richard Weizsacker, then President of Germany, speaking of the Holocaust said, "We cannot undo the past but we have to know the past and teach it to prevent such reoccurrences in the future." In 1998 in a concentrated three-week period before Rosh

Hashanah, a number of towns in Italy, including Reggio Emilia and Parma (source of Parmesan cheese), observed Jewish contributions to Italian life with readings, concerts, exhibits, and lectures by respected cultural figures including A. B. Yehoshua, the distinguished Israeli author. In Trieste, where only a thousand Jews still live, a week-long celebration of the city's Jewish history entitled "Shalom Trieste" took place with major exhibits on the evils of anti-Semitism.

The timing of the statements, confessions of sin, apologies, and requests for forgiveness leading up to and during celebration of jubilee year and beginning of a new millennium is historically important. Accompanied by constructive acts, these statements transcend the possible destructive conduct of cultists and predictions of Armageddon.

Doomsday cults have forewarned of ominous events in the millennium, of an apocalypse—the end of time, the end of Earth—producing fear that this period could represent a once-in-a-thousand year opportunity for such movements to vent anger upon society and governments. Doomsday cults have always had a special liking for predicting an impending cataclysm in a specific time frame. Words, statements, and acts of contrition by leaders of the Church have diminished fears of such destructive conduct.

The timing is all the more propitious for the Jewish community for there is new life in European Jewry. Countries of the former communist bloc are experiencing a visible Jewish renewal; many, particularly younger people are discovering and reclaiming their long-buried Jewish roots, openly declaring their Jewish identity in Poland, the Czech Republic, Slovakia, Hungary, Russia, and Bulgaria. Judaism is moving forward even in Germany, which has absorbed 70,000 Jewish immigrants from the former Soviet Union with many more coming. National Jewish organizations are training teachers, professionals, and voluntary leaders; centers of Jewish learning are being established. Hundreds of thousands remaining in Russia, Ukraine, and other countries carved out of the former Soviet Union are reopening synagogues and schools, rebuilding Jewish communities in places where Jewish thought, movement, and expression had been suppressed.

A BRIEF HISTORY OF ANTI-SEMITISM

Prejudice will not be eliminated swiftly. After being transmitted from generation to generation through the ages and becoming deeply embedded in the minds of men, it will not be exorcised quickly. Anti-Semitism existed among the Greeks, when Jewish monotheistic belief in one God clashed with Greek worship and belief in many gods; it continued into Roman times when Judaism was tolerated as an "ethnic" religion. Anti-Semitism proliferated with the advent of Christianity and the refusal by Jews to accept Jesus as the Messiah; it was strengthened by claims that Jews had killed Christ. Hate was transmitted by the Church and its followers from parents to children, and that hate deepened and evolved into the greatest hatred in human history. Though Jews suffered in Islam, where they were viewed as second-class people, Muslim hate did not reach Christian levels. After all, Jews were not accused of having killed Mohammed.

Whenever there was considerable disunity within the Christian church itself, the church leaders brought about unity by encouraging the persecution of Jews. Pope Urban II in November, 1095, called upon the kings and nobles of European Christendom to cease fighting each other and to join together to liberate Jerusalem and the Holy Land. As the Crusaders marched through Europe on the way to war with Islam, anti-Semitism reached a crescendo and tens of thousands of Jews were killed by Crusader mobs. Fantasies of Jewish conspiracies had risen, as had the myth of Jews murdering Christian children for religious reasons, intensifying the hatred of Jews. In the second millennium, long before the expulsion of the Jews of Spain with the Inquisition, Jews were expelled from England in 1290, not to return until the 17th century; France in 1306; Hungary in 1349; Austria in 1421; from Germany in the 14th, 15th, and 16th Centuries; from Lithuania in 1445, Portugal in 1497, from Russia in the 16th century; and Bohemia and Moravia in 1745 among other places.

DEVELOPING PREJUDICE

Prejudice is a child of ignorance. It often represents a negative opinion or idea about a group or its members formed without knowledge of the group or any individual. And so anti-Semitism occurred even in societies in which Jews were conspicuously absent. Chaucer's *Canterbury Tales* characterized Jews as ritual murderers. Shakespeare portrayed Jews negatively in the *Merchant of Venice* and other plays even though there were no Jews living in England and he had never met a Jew.

Prejudice feeds on societal stress. In the Middle Ages, masses of people died of bubonic plague for which the Jews were held responsible, though they themselves died of the disease along with other people. When the Polish economy was in disarray in 1998, the Jews, only 20,000 of them, the surviving remnant of the pre-Holocaust community of 3.5 million, were blamed. History's favorite scapegoat is the Jew.

Societal stress was very high in Germany after World War I. Extremely harsh peace terms imposed by the Allies resulted in economic disorganization, a 25% rate of unemployment, poverty, and humiliation. These conditions were fertile for revolution and dictatorship, as downtrodden people are susceptible to promises of prosperity with change—any change. As it had been possible to direct unhappiness toward scapegoats during the Black Death, so was it possible to do so between the two world wars. The Nazi party ascended as they directed unhappiness and hostility toward the Jews.

Sociologists and psychologists know that people are not born good or evil and that, regardless of their nature, human beings are conditioned by their experiences. People learn prejudice by living with it. Bigoted parents transmit bigoted ideas to children. Hatred is blind. Anti-Semitics do not see the object of their hatred as a human being. They do not see the Jew for what he or she is but only for what they perceive the Jew to be. Perception is reality. If in American society people are painted in negative, stereotypical terms (i.e. "blacks are shiftless, Hispanics are lazy") and no one reacts negatively, people assume what they hear is how things are supposed to be. People who would ordinarily be skeptical of grandiose charges are often swayed by them in bad times. The attitudes of people, their folkways, and their mores create a commonality in conduct and thought. After attitudes are formed, they are difficult to redirect. The Catholic Church was guilty of tolerating intolerance, which resulted in acceptance of intolerance by the people; the Church then became an accessory to horror.

Statements, apologies, expressions of guilt, and self-abnegation by Church leaders in eminent positions as are now taking place have been unknown in history. The Jewish attitude could easily be dismissive, but the statements we hear and read breathe light into the fundamental Jewish belief that the doors of reconciliation are never closed. To believe that we are entrapped in an eternal cycle of hatred and war is the essence of faithlessness. The essence of any faith is the renewability of the human spirit.

HEROES IN ACTION

A Jewish folk saying admonishes people to look for the good, not the evil. Thus it is necessary to be aware that even as Nazi Germany was inflicting the most unimaginably brutal crimes on the Jewish people, some Christians protected Jewish people, sometimes at the risk of their own lives.

Through heroic action in Denmark in 1943, nearly the entire Jewish population of that country was spirited off to Sweden by Danes, led in large part by Protestant pastors. According to Yehuda Bauer, during the Nazi rule of terror, 4,000 priests from all over Europe were murdered, though the Catholic Church in Germany, with its impressive membership of 33 million people, never publicly recognized that the defense of the Jews was a Christian duty.

A group called Zegota (Polish underground) was organized by Henryk Wolinski and is said to have saved more than 4,000 children and adults in Warsaw and Krakow. Otto Busse, director of a German factory in Bialystok (near Treblinka), smuggled food past guards into the ghetto and provided supplies for Jewish fighters during the ghetto rebellion. Irene Gootupdike, a 17-year-old Polish-Catholic girl, forced to work in a laundry for a group of Germans and as a housekeeper for a senior officer, hid twelve Jews in the home of that officer and smuggled food and supplies to the people in the ghetto. Anna Shimaite, a Lithuanian, served as a messenger for Jews in the ghetto, collecting their clothes and valuables, which she delivered to them along with forged papers with which Jews could pass themselves off as Gentiles.

In France, Archbishop Jules Gerard Scliege of Toulouse demanded that parish priests help Jews and smuggled them across borders to areas where they could be safe. Sister Marie Lepetit of Toulouse, just 20 years old, saved many Jewish children and said simply afterwards, "We had no choice—we could not let them die." Andre Herscovici of Gimonia, Belgium ran a Catholic boarding school where he placed and saved four to five children a day.

Clearly, fear played a role in limiting the number of heroic acts by people, yet many, at grave risk, helped Jews, heeding the religious and human admonition to save life. They rejected the trumpery, rationalizations, and fear used by most religious leaders to explain their lack of action, which resulted in having only slightly more than 1% of the Jewish population in Poland success-fully hidden in Polish ethnic areas.

POPE JOHN XXIII

The most helpful of all churchmen to the Jewish people during the Holocaust was undoubtedly Monsignor Angelo Roncalli, later Pope John XXIII, a revered and beloved man. The Vatican Council convened by him in 1962 revolutionized the Catholic Church by adopting Nostra Aetate, the document that repudiated Catholic teaching that Jews were collectively responsible for Jesus's death. The move taken recently by Pope John Paul II to beatify Pope John XXIII as part of the process toward sainthood is, as would be expected, enthusiastically welcomed by informed Jews and humanists generally.

When the Nazis demanded that Bulgaria destroy all of its Jews, John XXIII, then Monsignor Roncalli, apostolic delegate to Turkey, intervened and threat-ened King Boris of Bulgaria with the "punishment of God." Orders to deport the Jews were canceled and 25,000 Bulgarian Jews were saved. Roncalli arranged for thousands of Jews to obtain certificates of baptism, used only for the purpose of snatching them from death. Later as Papal Nuncio in Budapest, Hungary, Monsignor Roncalli is said to have issued more than 15,000 "safe conduct" passages to Jews, aided by Bishop William Aporgyor.

Expressions of sadness and contrition by high members of the Catholic Church are significant, particularly for believers, for the Catholic Church is one in which centralized authority is vested first of all in the Pope but also in cardinals, bishops, and priests. Silence by the Vatican during the Holocaust influenced the conduct of the Catholics of Germany, approximately half the population. Silence helped produce silence, influencing people to inaction, diminishing the number of acts of heroism that could have saved more lives. Similarly, the words of the present, six decades later, can mold attitudes; a mighty effort may at least moderate history's longest hatred—hatred of the Jews.

The act of Pope John XXIII in convening the second Vatican council in 1962, repudiating the notion of collective Jewish guilt for the death of Jesus, was a significant beginning, followed as it has been by Christianity's acknowledgement of its own errors, apologies, and pleas for forgiveness and rapprochement. As each gesture, each statement over the last 2,000 years contributed to the creation of a climate of hate, so can positive statements, gestures, and acts affect people in the future.

We live in a time of rapid advance in communications, heavily used by political candidates for national and world positions. Business enterprises invest huge sums to sell their wares. These methods of communication can also be used to teach tolerance and love for one's fellow human being.

Archbishop Weakland stated that he was not expecting his words to have an immediate impact given the long history of antagonism, but words, he said, are a first step toward a "spirit of healing." The Archbishop said he regards his own statement as only a beginning. Edmund Burke admonished, "Nobody makes a greater mistake than he who does nothing because he can only do a little." The Archbishop's admission of error and sin, concurrent with apologies and pleas of other Church leaders, including the Pope, as well as heads of state and other forces, represent more than a little. These words create perceptions that lead to deeds.

History tells us that the most effective prophets work to make their prophecies come true. Our Jewish faith teaches us that which will happen must be made to happen. The statements, apologies, and thoughts of friendship come at a uniquely significant time, a jubilee year coinciding with the beginning of a third millennium for the Christian church. The change taking place is far more than a little beginning; it may herald glad tidings of better times for the Jewish people and all of humanity.

PART III:

LEADING THE COMMUNITY

THE EXECUTIVE AS A LEADER

Keynote address to the National Institute for Executives,
Council of Jewish Federation and Welfare Funds in Tamarack, NY.

August 1967

Who are we? We are organizers, recruiters, teachers, mentors, community planners, negotiators, and trainers of leaders. Sometimes we are whipping boys for agencies, for leaders, and for other professionals.

And we are diplomats. We negotiate with all kinds of agencies, local and national. We have learned that it is sometimes necessary to be watchful, to guard our flanks, for we know full well, without being at all paranoid, that in the confines of some offices of agencies, even some to which we are devoted and for which we raise money, someone who's displeased may be calculating ways of getting the best of us. We know full well that some organizations that we work hard to support would nevertheless weaken the fabric of what we build. There are those who do not welcome the existence of a central organization responsible for any form of oversight of communal services that does not suit their purposes. Such people would describe their conduct differently. Professionals express support for the idea of federation modified by their need to do whatever they must for the organization that employs them, pays them; volunteers express support for the organization that honors them by election to positions of directors or officers, in effect complicating a true community spirit.

Sometimes I think it takes more skill to deal with some Jewish agencies than is needed by international diplomats deciding the fate of all humankind.

Who has not at some point listened to the layperson of strength and influence who has uttered words such as these, "If you don't do as I wish"; or to the big giver who has said, "If you won't allocate money as I wish"; or to the rabbi with a following; or to the executive of a national agency with local support, "If you can't give us. . . ." You finish the sentence. All of this prompted a most sophisticated voluntary leader—a big giver, campaign chair, and top national leader—to say to me, "You are in the hardest business in the world." And, that is not only his opinion, it is also mine.

Let's look at this hardest business in the world together and ask ourselves why we work hard to recruit, place, create, develop, orient, teach, and counsel leaders; to raise money and organize; and to engage in sometimes terribly sensitive and tense diplomacy. To do all of this well requires strength and courage. No one can do it without a sense of mission.

Let's look at what we do and at the instrument, federation, in which we believe. Let us ask ourselves why we do this work in a world filled with so many problems to which we could direct our energies. Tenacious, intractable problems confront us all over the world. We have the power within our hands to destroy ourselves and the world at any moment. As Jews we have the added challenge of making our Jewishness more meaningful.

Our great rabbis have always insisted that the task of people here on earth is to perfect the lot of humankind. We believe that the noblest work of people is perfecting society. Judaism contends that the world can progress—that despair and pessimism must be pushed aside. We declare that perfecting the community is a central task for each human being. We feel certain that a better community can be obtained, and we strive for it.

In this tough world in which people are set against people, the idea of federation has a special attraction. Somehow it seems and feels as though Hillel must have been thinking of us when he called upon each person to be for the other as well as for him- and herself. And Maimonides must have been thinking of ideas underlying Jewish federations when he said, "It is the duty of man to associate himself with the community." And so with John Donne when he wrote that no man is an island and Einstein when he spoke of his interdependence with all of humankind with whom he was intertwined.

The Executive—Rating Ourselves

Each of us would do well to examine our communities by asking some key questions: Do we have good participation from what we would regard as a logical cross-section of the community? Do capable people accept communal responsibility? Have provisions been made for orderly transitions in leadership? Is new leadership constantly coming into the picture? Are there opportunities for new people to give of themselves? Can we say that those who work and lead today represent advancement as compared with a year ago? Five years ago? Do we know who our leaders will be next year? And the year after that? How much money is raised—do we believe it is a satisfactory result, one upon which we can build? Are we convinced that we can do better next year? The year after that?

I know of a community that for more than 20 years had inept executives. The shallow understanding of voluntary leaders and lack of skillful professionals brought that community to near ruin. If that community had no professional at all, it could at least begin as virgin territory. If no professional had been there, at the very least volunteers could begin without disrespect for professionalism.

A lesson that each of us should learn from experience is that each person has some control over his or her own destiny, that the individual is the agent not the victim of that destiny. It is useless to brood over lack of communal unity, when there are so many who support the principles we stand for.

The demands upon federations, as central instruments, to plan and direct services, to administer, and to raise money cannot ever be borne by executives alone. Those demands can be satisfied only with the participation of many people who share our concerns, have knowledge, and know how to lead. A sound professional leader must see to it that there is a concerned, devoted, respected voluntary leadership. The name of this game is involvement. The world, the country, the community, everything is only as good as its leadership.

I hear so many plaintive professional cries of a lack of leadership and often think of them as mirroring inadequacies of the complaining executive. There are people of good will with ability and a desire to give of themselves in every community—the kind of people who can and will be the leaders of today and

107

tomorrow if only given the opportunity. The people are there—they are more available to us than to any other professionals. Our people have a tradition of giving of themselves, of uniting in the face of difficulty and oppression. Our campaigns for funds give people feelings of satisfaction and provide a sense for them of worthwhileness—of helping, building, and saving lives. We must see to it that people of varying views, interested in Jewish life, are brought together, for a common cause. The federation executive is given an opportunity to encourage these people to develop within themselves a sense of belonging. All people have that need, a need to be a part of something. People are not islands, isolated from each other. When we are involved in providing opportunities for people to work within the Jewish community, we contribute to Jewish solidarity and survival.

How often we hear welcome expressions of appreciation on the part of voluntary participants, "Thanks for letting me be a part of this" or "I didn't know the federation or Welfare Fund did all these things; I'm so glad I'm part of it now" or "I'd like to be on this committee or that one."

The antithesis of the good community with year-round involvement is the one in which small boards of directors make decisions quickly, neatly, and efficiently as in a private enterprise. The backward campaign for funds is chaired in that low-quality federation by an unlucky fellow, who is told that it is his turn to take the job. It's the one in which the campaign usually raises the same or slightly less than the year before, after which a small group comes together and allocates money, based on little knowledge. The group laments the poor quality of gifts unrelated to peoples' affluence and far short of the amount required to meet community needs and responsibilities. That is not building, planning, and working; it is resignation to failure, whether in the small nonprofessionalized community or in the large one.

IDENTIFYING AND DEVELOPING LEADERSHIP

The leadership of a generation ago emerged with little training. They were caring, responsible people. We need those qualities. But now we need people with more understanding of the complexity of services, of relationships of American and world Jewry with Israel, and with sensibilities to the frequent rivalry of agencies with each other. We need leaders, diplomatic people able to encourage cooperation. That kind of leadership can come about only through planned programs to which we give impetus.

The quality of leadership development programs in various cities depends largely on what we do to identify potential leaders who share community-building objectives. Our job is to identify these potential leaders and to encourage their involvement.

There is some logical order to leadership development. It requires a substantial backdrop in which community members understand that we believe that the enterprise belongs to them, that they have a major voice in its organization, in the operation of its agencies and institutions, and in the services for people including themselves. There are ways to create that understanding, not just through publicity but through year-round grassroots contact.

We hear so much in these days of emphasis on Jewish survival, about the dearth of real knowledge in most communities. It is very good to have leaders with fine Jewish backgrounds, but I have observed that often people who are learned in Jewish history, sometimes even religiously committed, are not altogether willing to commit deeds in keeping with their presumed creeds. Yet, large numbers of men and women who have been deprived of suitable education, perceived by others as being uninformed, carry on work out of concern and a love for humanity and the Jewish people. Many such people hunger for information. In the final analysis, that which we do depends upon heart as well as knowledge, and the heart that helps a person to be passionate about what we stand for motivates him or her to seek knowledge.

OUR MORE OPEN SOCIETY

Our society is opening. Jewish people discriminated against in the past, unwelcome on boards of directors of all kinds of civic organizations, now are welcomed, even sought after. Prejudice is diminishing. Israel's image has ascended as a result of its extraordinary defeat of confrontational states that would destroy her in the Six-Day War, just over two months ago. The spirit of Jewish people throughout the world has been raised; the identity with Israel has deepened. In this more open society, non-Jews become members of

Jewish community centers, our Jewish Vocational Services serve large numbers of people irrespective of religion or race, especially people with challenging problems, and predominant numbers of patients in our Jewish hospitals are not Jews.

It becomes all the more necessary to keep our wits about us and to help the volunteer understand the sense of mission of the Jewish community. If we serve ourselves well, we will have a capacity to serve society better, as we lash out against oppression.

We professionals are jugglers. We bring together people with all shades of opinion. We could help even some who are hostile and highly competitive with each other to set aside these negative feelings and to substitute for them a bit of love. The sound and strong professional helps bring such people together in a common cause.

The leadership of today is an educated group, indigenous primarily to the American soil, and its members want to understand what they are involved in and what we ask of them. Leadership training in this day must be precisely what the words imply; real training. It cannot come from an inspired talk to lift the spirits once a year to a worker on the eve of a campaign. Inspiration today must come from knowledge, involvement, and a sense of identification. We need to create leadership groups, consisting of people carefully recruited, who are among those we are confident can and will give of themselves.

TEST YOURSELF AS A LEADER

Ask yourself these questions. Are there leaders in my communities who were not leaders a few years ago and whose evolution into leadership I had something to do with? Ask yourself another question—are these people who are leaders better because of me? Did I do something to make them better leaders? Now ask another question, are these people unaware of the effect I have had upon them? For if they are, it is the best reflection on you, for it means that they believe with all of their hearts that they are there as a result only of their own interests and their own labor. It means that your cause has also become theirs, a prelude to this kind of commitment.

From time to time I look at photographs of volunteers at meetings and I ask myself—are those who lead now more able, better versed, a more dedicated group than those who led before, and if not, why not, and how did I err?

A good community should have the problem of having too many people who are impatient to become the campaign chair or the president. The good community is one in which people seek the opportunity to serve in the largest possible ways.

CAMPAIGNING IN 1968—AN OPPORTUNITY

I know that there is a feeling of confidence that 1968 may be an easy campaign year. After all, did we not just have the most extraordinary fundraising experience in history with an outpouring of wealth in response to the Six-Day War? What an expression of commitment, of American Jewish solidarity with Israel. The emotional peaks that our people reached, the mass participation of Jews whom some of us had never heard of or from, the rush of activity, the offers to serve, the long lists of people offering their blood, as well as their dollars were unparalleled. Now what we are called upon to do is to take hold of this upsurge of involvement and to incorporate it into our existing campaigns so that our communities may have stable, strong forces for organized Jewish life. There are some extraordinary opportunities open to us, which are almost heaven-sent for some communities.

But let us think back now on those events. On June 3, 1967, some of us were gathered together at a meeting in New York at which the Israel Emergency Fund was born. The noose around Israel's throat was tightening. Remember the impassioned words of Louis Pincus when he said that Israel's choice was slow strangulation or war. Remember your feeling, if you were there the next morning, when Lewis Weinstein shouted, "Am Yisrael Chai— the people of Israel live, and they will live." What were you feeling? What were you really thinking? You feared for Israel and her people. You knew that overwhelming forces were poised with daggers pointed at Israel's throat, that people whom you regarded as bone of your bone, the remnants that we had helped save, that the Israel for which some of us have worked so hard and with which we said so often our destinies are intertwined, that all of this could be destroyed. Our pain, our agony, the fears of hundreds of thousands of Jews, the last-chance feeling, the guilt in the hearts of people who had done so little, the pride of those who have done so much—all combined and resulted in an outpouring of money. For what else could we do? And then there was the glory of Israel's achievement and the remaking of history and the charging of the air we breathe with an emotion that filled Jews throughout the world. Jews felt as one with Jews—even in the Soviet Union—even in places where Jews were suppressed as Jews.

People poured out their money, dramatically demonstrating that Jews care about their fellow Jews. The five-dollar giver gave a thousand, the hundred-dollar giver gave fifteen hundred, and the three thousand dollar giver gave forty thousand.

Our country identified itself with Israel in its struggle. We had all kinds of strange new bedfellows, even some whose kinship with us was startling.

But let us face the fact that before this provocative situation in Israel, some of the annual welfare fund campaigns were running out of gas. Communities that were doing poorly for a number of years were engaged in self-examination. Some such federations have now been given a new life. But it is conceivable that the James Bondish idea is correct and that "You only live twice." Some communities had better grasp that new life. Remember, Israel may not be at war next year—there might be peace. Isn't that what we wish for? We must prefer peace to Arab obdurateness, and we hope for a great program of rehabilitation for the Arab refugees led by a creative Israel concerned with Arab homelessness. All of this is not an easy task, burdened as it is with the hate of two decades and the dead of three wars.

All communities should have learned from the Israel Emergency Fund experience, even those that raise the most money and have the best per capita income. Clearly, no one has ever done the maximum job. Clearly, there was more money available in every community. There has been no cease-fire on human needs, and so there can be no cease-fire on campaign planning, development, and promotion. The job will be to act quickly and to re-evaluate and to restructure and to plan anew.

But it is the community with the relatively poor income with which I am most concerned. A community raising only ten dollars per capita or twenty or thirty is in trouble. When a community deteriorates over a number of years, then the Israel Emergency Fund means all the more. It means opportunity; it means that circumstances beyond our control propelled a generosity that we may not have imagined possible or that at least had never been realized. These are the communities in which some quick evolution is possible. If we do our job well, we will learn more about the givers who gave and why they gave and what their interests are. We will explore quickly methods of bringing them into the fold. I envy the executive in an underdeveloped community who can experience a sense of mission and extraordinary achievement. It is like being able to go into a new society or a new emerging nation and feel a constructive revolutionary process.

But remember that the function of history is to help us chart the future as a result of our understanding of the past. In 1948, Israel became a state. Large sums of money poured forth, and those committed to the idea of Israel as well as those who only thought it right that the Jews still living in displaced persons camps be given a home gave their money. And in 1949, there was no war and in the face of great need campaigns fell and many communities began a steep decline. The exceptions were the well-organized and well-led communities. History tells us that the well-organized communities were strengthened in 1948, and those communities went forth and continued to raise more money each year. Those who did not assess the situation well, who did not create a planned involvement of their people, who did not work on the creation of good relationships between the various elements in the community, who did not build on the spirit and excitement of that moment let their communities slide into deep valleys from their high peaks.

Today, the executive leading a community that is in a deep abyss must understand that without quick action the community will return to its previous low levels. But if they work quickly and effectively they can lead the community to change. Do so before the ardor cools. Communities are built by the very moment. Time must not be lost.

THE PROFESSIONAL AND THE VOLUNTEER

Presented at the General Assembly of the Council of Jewish Federations in Dallas.

November 1977

The search for sound and wise leadership is as old as the first cooperative venture entered into by human beings. The world, a country, and a community are only as good as their leadership. Without high-quality leadership, the Jewish community and its service organizations do not thrive.

For a community to progress, it must be led by people who have appropriate knowledge, organize well, apply reason and logic in the planning of communal services, raise money effectively, and manage it efficiently. Philanthropy in America is big business, involving 30 million people in social, religious, and political organizations as volunteers. The well-being of millions of people and sometimes their very lives depend on the quality of our work. The conduct of so vital an enterprise requires skill and devotion.

THE EVOLUTION OF THE JEWISH VOLUNTEER

By 1900, the rapidly growing Jewish population of the United States had reached approximately one million. Because the primarily immigrant population had too many needs for volunteers to handle alone, people were employed and paid to do much of the work. The Jewish community professional came into existence, carrying out necessary duties on behalf of the Jewish people, with oversight by volunteers who made decisions based on their understanding and sometimes simply the recommendations of the professionals.

Volunteers manifested their concern for their fellow human beings by giving money and by creating the organizations run by the professionals that provided shelter for the homeless, jobs, and aid for immigrants. They distributed financial assistance to Jews with whom they identified and also, in part, out of the concern that dependency by Jews on public funds could evoke a negative response in a Christian-dominated American society. The big givers were generous, caring people, by and large immigrants of an earlier time who had made good. They were followed by their sons and daughters who learned from the examples provided by their elders to help their fellow Jews. The less affluent gave modest sums so they too could participate in acts of tzedakah. It was simpler then for the professional—he dealt with a few people who gave most of the money, made the decisions, and that was that.

The cataclysmic Holocaust, followed by the birth of Israel, dictated a reordering of Jewish priorities: first, physical survival, and then spiritual and emotional survival. Jewish education for children was emphasized as a means of perpetuating the Jewish people. There developed an understanding of the special relationship between Israel and the Jewish Diaspora. The primary decision-makers in communities had been men; in time, women were welcomed into leadership circles, and gender as a factor in attaining leadership positions diminished in importance. As women's movements seek equality with men, I'm reminded of realities in my own community in which I've often questioned whether men could lead equally with women.

The staff members of federations in earlier times were often there by happenstance. They were frequently people without special Jewish knowledge or commitment, who worked for Jewish agencies because they were the best jobs available. After World War II, there was a growing recognition that Jewish communal professionals needed to be well trained and Jewishly knowledgeable. Requirements came to include not only advanced professional training but also participation in continuing education and a commitment to Jewish values based on history and tradition.

The nature of the volunteers changed as well. They are more Americanized, less acquainted with authentic Jewish life, far better educated secularly than their predecessors and sometimes are inspired by visits to Israel. These more sophisticated volunteers are better able to develop intellectually and to be affected by Jewish culture. Living in a social climate more open to Jewish people than ever before, Jewish volunteers now sit on the boards of museums, symphony orchestras, and prestigious civic organizations. Jews who were not welcome in these institutions are now their presidents and leaders. It is as though civic leaders are applying the words of Rabbi Nahman of Bratslav, who wrote two hundred years ago, "When a person is able to take abuse with a smile, that person is worthy to become a leader." Yet many caring Jews, now very much active in these endeavors of the total society, are no less involved in the Jewish community, demonstrating a conscious choice and real commitment to Jewish life.

Because of the ascendancy of federations, the idea of community has taken hold more among Jews than among any segment of American society. It is no longer each agency for itself, like businesses competing in a marketplace. The sophisticated volunteer considers the federation to be the most efficient system known to meet communal needs and problems by coordinating and binding humanistic impulses together. People of vision see federations collectively as a continental instrument through which people and communities collaborate to deal with matters of concern to Jewish people everywhere.

However, any assumption that the advanced concept of federation is wholeheartedly supported by all elements in the community represents wishful thinking. Our belief in the value of an organized community and a coherent, harmonious examination and collective determination of needs and responsibilities is not enthusiastically welcomed in all circles. If it were, then we would not have the present abundance of campaigns for funds, some of which are disruptive of community order and some of which are even conducted by federation-supported local and national agencies. In addition, there would be more complete, enthusiastic, compliance with the progressive federation ideal of community planning. The pursuit of a healthy cooperative spirit makes it essential that those who lead the federation, volunteers—professionals alike, be people of tact and diplomacy.

LAY-PROFESSIONAL RELATIONSHIP

Today's professionals and volunteers choose to become active in Jewish community life because of their Jewish commitment, ideals and beliefs. They see in their involvement a means of expressing their devotion to a cause.

Board members and officers are legally responsible in every way for the acts and conduct of the organization. The board establishes policies, oversees expenditures and services provided, and is responsible for reporting to the community. In years gone by, the role of the professional was limited to implementing the decisions made by lay leaders.

In contrast, today's professionals play a major role in the development of policy from the moment that they collect and present information to the volunteer leader—faithfully, as most do, although sometimes inaccurately, either wittingly or unwittingly. I have known executives who presented material, made up of thickets of jargon, described platitudinously as "transparent," yet knowing it to be quite opaque and sometimes purposely so. When information is presented in nebulous ways, people who do not understand are often reluctant to raise questions, lest they seem uninformed or ignorant. The volunteer board members in this position, fearful of exposing a lack of knowledge in the presence of others, usually are unaware that others are also perplexed and so all remain quiet. Questions are not posed, the matter not clarified, yet the minutes record the issues as presented, endorsed, and accepted. This becomes a serious shortfall in the governance of a community, with the responsible volunteer board having a diminished capacity to act, ceding responsibility to the professional.

When a professional works in such ways, the federation's effectiveness is reduced. In contrast, when issues are understood and truly transparent, the federation inevitably will have a higher quality of leaders in terms of knowledge, interest, and willingness to give of themselves. When the executive lacks knowledge, or purposely colors information, volunteers remain uninformed or misinformed and lose interest, and the community suffers.

In the ideal partnership, the professional is not the only source of information; informed volunteers may have preconceived ideas of their own, shaped by their own experiences and information available from other sources. Volunteers and professionals share in informing the public and in transmitting data as a basis for decisions, policymaking, and practices and thus work as a team implementing policies and achieving goals.

When a voluntary board thinks it makes all the decisions, with the role of the executive only to provide information—then look out. When an executive thinks that it is his or her prerogative to make all the decisions—also look out. When volunteers and professionals share information, and jointly arrive at a decision, that is partnership. The assumption that the professional is just a gatherer of information for the volunteer who then makes decisions is a theory often killed by the facts.* Though voluntary leaders are responsible for policy and decision-making, the professional, has a substantial input through information gathering and presentation. When information, skewed by the professional's bias, whether purposefully or not, is presented as fact, and so accepted, the professional becomes more then just a partner.

Good volunteers are upright people of high ideals who give generously of themselves and of their money. They view giving money as an act of tzedakah, as a holy act of redemption. They know that in prayer, the Jew uses the word *Kadosh*, holy, holy, holy, and that holiness consists not of prayer alone but also of holy conduct, as manifested through acts of tzedakah. True leaders are generous not only with financial resources but also with their ideas, labor, and energy. They bring to mind a line in Walt Whitman's "Leaves of Grass": "Behold, I do not give a little cry, when I give, I give myself." Maimonides wrote, "Take away generosity and our earth would be a tomb."

True voluntary leaders have a role in resolving questions and issues and thus need to be knowledgeable. They should be expected to continue to learn as they serve, and the professional, who must in part be a teacher, is expected to help enhance their knowledge. No person has ever been so well informed as not to be able to gain new knowledge as a result of age and experience. Time is a school in which we learn. As Samuel Johnson wrote in 1759, "Integrity, without knowledge, is weak and useless, and knowledge without integrity is dangerous and dreadful."

THE PRESIDENT–EXECUTIVE RELATIONSHIP

The elected, voluntary, unpaid president is the principal leader of the fed-

---

* Thomas Huxley refers to "the slaying of a beautiful hypothesis by ugly fact." in biogenenesis and Abiogenenesis.

eration, and the community. This is the most complex of all community voluntary assignments, for it requires an awareness of a variety of services and agencies, not only those within the community itself but also of national organizations to which each community is related. In a federation, the president must also have some familiarity with developments in Jewish life around the world, especially Israel. The board of directors, officers, and especially the president have the responsibility for hiring the executive; they are thus collectively an employer.

The executive has the major responsibility for hiring, guiding, and supervising other professionals. He or she also has substantial influence by helping determine which lay leaders are given major decision-making power. By giving advice on board committee composition, particularly the nominating committee, the executive may influence the selection of people whose duties include oversight of his or her work.

All effective professionals engage constantly in a search for the best possible leaders, people of excellence who will not automatically agree with their points of view and wishes, or be supportive of their manner of work. Fearful, insecure, inadequate, and manipulative professionals sometimes use stratagems to prevent the selection of volunteers with authority who hold views different from their own. In contrast, worthy, informed professionals of integrity know that fallibility exists within everyone, seek out the best leadership, and accept the risks that they and voluntary leaders with whom they may differ will work effectively together, with mutual respect.

In places where there is a dearth of voluntary involvement, in which leadership development programs are non-existent or flawed, it is sometimes necessary to co-opt a reluctant president to preside at meetings—following the agenda, notes prepared, and guidance of the executive. Such a president may be an asset in some ways because of prestige or status, but he or she is a president in name only and the professional is often the de facto president. In such circumstances the president often permits the executive to make decisions in the president's name with the president gaining no new knowledge as a result—a situation incongruent with the perceived responsibilities and status of a genuine communal leader. One good measure of an executive's worth is how much other people know, learn, how they work and how they lead.

Public Presence

The term of a president is limited in time, in contrast to the executive whose tenure has no specific time limit. During his or her time-limited term in office, the president is expected to have the most visible community presence of anyone. However, sometimes professionals, who enjoy a center stage profile, fill the community role meant for the president. When a too busy president, with little time, remains low profile, some professionals are all too eager to fill the vacuum. A president who does not have enough time to gain in knowledge deprives the community of high-quality leadership. Francis Bacon put it simply when he said, "knowledge itself is power."

I have often observed that some professionals would benefit from a good dose of anonymity. The mark of good professional leaders is their capacity to influence, to teach, to inform, and to help others look good, rather than to seek public notice for themselves. Professionals should remember that modesty is a very high virtue and that it is not looking good that is important, but rather doing good. There is a cogent Jewish folk saying, "Fools see people's clothes; wise individuals see people's spirit."

A primary basis for determining the effectiveness of a professional is the quality and number of leaders in the community and the depth of their knowledge. The principled executive of integrity is most satisfied knowing that leaders have grown in knowledge, which serves as the basis for their participation and decision making. It becomes evident that decisions are made thoughtfully.

Consider these words on leadership of the Chinese philosopher Lao-Tse (circa 565 BCE):

A leader is best
When people barely know he exists.
Not so good when people obey and acclaim him,

But of a good leader, who talks little,
When his work is done, his aim fulfilled,
They will say, "We did this ourselves."

What is most needed is teamwork between the president and the executive, with each discharging their responsibilities. The right hand should know at all times what the left hand is doing. Clapping with one hand only, produces nothing.

PRINCIPLES FOR TODAY'S VOLUNTEERS AND PROFESSIONALS

The Holocaust and the birth of Israel ushered in a historic era of fundraising. More money was needed to save refugees, help people make aliyah to Israel, to come to the United States and other countries, and to share in building Jewish communities worldwide. Nothing could be done without large sums of money. That required a new kind of community power structure filled by people who understood the need for the money and were prepared to give generously and to ask others to do so. It called for people of vision, with an ability to look ahead and anticipate problems and needs that might arise. A capacity to see what might not be visible to other people was needed. There was a new emphasis on social planning, soon to be called community planning. That planning required an understanding of human need and an appreciation of the concept of community. It called for togetherness. It meant that l'dor l'dor, from generation to generation, could not just be a slogan, that knowledge of the past, which produced the present and would mold the future, was necessary.

The lay-professional relationship should be guided by these principles:

- For voluntary leaders to give of themselves, the activity must provide a sense of worthwhileness and achievement.

- Volunteers should not be asked to do more than they can do.

- The duties volunteers are asked to perform should be in keeping with their interests.

- Volunteers must be confident that the enterprise with which they are involved is well managed.

- Every human being needs a sense of identity. The identity of the volunteer should be highlighted.

To determine their understanding and commitment, potential volunteers should be asked these three simple questions:

1. Do you respect the professional's role as being important?

2. Would you encourage your son or daughter to become a staff member of a Jewish federation, knowing what they would contend with?

3. If you yourself were in a professional position, do you believe you would feel a sense of acceptable status?

In turn, the professional could be asked these questions:

1. If you were a business person, doctor, accountant, or lawyer, would you choose to be a volunteer?

2. Would you do these things as a volunteer avocation, not as a vocation?

3. Do you believe that through voluntary work you could help make the community better and make a contribution to the world around you?

CONCLUSION

We live in a complex, often troubled world in which person is often set against person; in which the young struggle and rebel against their elders; and in which people of different races, groups, and religious beliefs and of different nations clash with and war against each other. In this kind of world, the good person seeks opportunities to love instead of hate, to cooperate rather than compete, to build rather than to tear down, to hallow human life and not to destroy it, to create hope where there is hopelessness.

There are many people in the world who need hopeful, positive approaches to life. That is particularly true of the Jews, an ancient people who have suffered so much to survive. Humanistic as well as religious admonitions call on us to hallow life and to make it worth living here on earth, in the here and now. Much that is good in this world grows from the sources of our faith, which calls upon us to strive constantly for a better world for all people. The federation is an instrument for unity. It binds together and teaches people to care about each other. It is an instrument through which people take strength from each other.

The authentic federation volunteer is conditioned to think in terms of what is good for all of the Jewish people, not just a segment of it. The volunteer and the professional work together to give meaning to Jewish prayers and hopes. There is a talmudic principle, "Man should perform righteous deeds, even if he does so only for ulterior motives because by doing so, he may learn to do the right thing for its own sake." We have gone far beyond that, for we think of our survival and our own worthwhileness as a people, as being good not only for ourselves, but for all the world.

Both the volunteer and the professional should feel that they enrich themselves by what they do. They recognize that the winter of old age can be long and hard for those who cannot look back upon enriching experiences. Gandhi wrote, "Man becomes great exactly in the degree in which he works for the welfare of his fellow men." None of us has the power to determine the length of life, but each has the capacity to give depth and meaning to that life. We have an obligation to use our time well. Good volunteers and good professionals hallow their lives by intelligent use all the days of their years.

A NOBILITY OF LEADERSHIP
UNFORGETTABLE PEOPLE—EULOGIES

An Explanatory Note

Milwaukee has been known for its leaders—society's nobility. There were many masterful leaders in the decades past and there are now. I would list many, but that could be bad manners for I could inadvertently miss a few, and if I were to list only a few, I could offend many, those present and the families of those passed. This chapter consists only of my feelings of three people expressed in eulogies I was called on to most painfully deliver at the ends of their lives. These people are representative within us of the nobility of the spirit of voluntary leadership. They inspired us. Their lives were blessings. Their deeds live on. They are remembered.

ANN AGULNICK
February 20, 1992

Truth, dignity, integrity, generosity, friendship, and humility—these values describe Ann through all of the days of her years. Ann had a strong conscience. She knew that by living in accordance with that powerful conscience, she would build good memories. Because she lived that way, we now have good memories of her.

ANN AS A LEADER

Ann was a leader from her youth to now, holding leadership positions in the 1930s, 1940s, 1950s, 1960s, 1970s, and 1980s. There was never a hiatus in her devotion to the Jewish community, to Israel, and to human welfare. She was an officer of the Jewish Federation in the 1940s long before it was fashionable for women to occupy positions of such status. She chaired federation budget committees and planning committees. She and a few other women of greatness founded the year-round Women's Division of the federation in the 1950s, of which she served as President and Campaign Chair. She was the president of Hadassah and a member of boards of many worthwhile agencies. When the Israel Bonds organization came into being in 1951, she chaired it. She was the only woman in all of America in such a position, and she helped create one of the most productive of all bond organizations. She strengthened the connection between Israel and the Diaspora.

Ann dignified every office and gave dignity to every organization with which she was associated. She never sought honor; she simply behaved honorably. Ann believed in doing the deed for the deed itself—not for the honor.

A community has many leaders. Some become role models, but Ann was the role model for role models—the mentor who mentored the mentors. If I weep, it is not me alone. If you hear a sob, it is not mine; it is from people over the decades, in so many of the years of our lives. It is from the hundreds directly touched by Ann, as well as the thousands on whom Ann's life had an effect. She was a symbol of life.

ANN AS A FUNDRAISER

We have, all of us, been involved in raising money for good causes. I have been raising funds for a very long time, and I have given advice on fundraising in many cities, countries, and continents. The best campaign team I've ever known was Ann Agulnick and Esther Cohen. People gave more money and were thankful to Esther and Ann for helping them feel good about doing what was right. They never pressed for money—they didn't need to. They convinced others by their sincerity. They never glorified in the amounts of money they had raised—only in the good that was done with it.

ANN AS A TEACHER AND STUDENT

Many of us learned from Ann. We think of her as a teacher, but she was always a student. She knew enough to know how much more there is to learn, so she continued to learn every day of her life. There was a human weakness that Ann could never comprehend—that was the love of ease. She just never quit and was never complacent about knowledge. She conveyed information to those who lead and would lead.

ANN'S ATTITUDES ON AGING

Ann lived for more than 90 years, but she was not old. In 1992, she was as young in imagination, in thought, as she was in 1972 or in 1952 or in 1932. Ann was a cheerful nonagenarian. She was 90 years young—that is far more cheerful than to be 30 years old. Nobody grows old only by living a number of years; people grow old by deserting their ideals. Yet, when Ann was still young in body, she was already old in knowledge.

Although she may have thought of death, she didn't dwell on it. She knew that there is something as inevitable as death, and that is life. She knew that if she constantly feared death, she would be unable to enjoy life.

She lived by the philosophy that the purpose of life is not just happiness but worthwhileness. People have no control over the length of their lives, but they have the freedom to determine its width and depth. Ann knew that. She never stopped reaching out to others. She acted with integrity—never, never with malice.

ANN AND PEOPLE

Ann respected people—the little person as well as the big. She was never obsequious with those perceived to be the powerful. She was equally respectful of the humble. She never hurt anybody knowingly. She never took advantage of anyone for personal gain. She was strong—not tough. Because she was big, she took on the big job, and because she had humility, she took on the little job for which she never felt too big. Perhaps the worst sin in life is to know right and not to do it. Ann knew that. She did what was right.

ANN AS A WOMAN

Ann achieved equal status with men as a leader long ago. When I met Ann 46 years ago, I knew of no man who would regard her as less than he. Within her, there was a synthesis of status with stature, but she was unconcerned with status. She was never threatening. She knew that men of quality are not threatened by equality for women. Equal status is achieved by the exercise of equal weight. Ann carried equal weight.

Many years ago, women—among them Ann—helped create a superb year-round federation Women's Division for the community. Men of understanding, who worked with these women, knew that if they worked with them they would reach not only women but also men and even children, and the community would become a better place.

ON MORALS, ETHICS, AND STRENGTH

There is a prayer that concludes with the words, "My God, keep my tongue from evil—my lips from speaking guile." I never heard Ann impugn anyone's integrity. I never heard her speak evil. She never compromised her principles.

Ann was a lesson in human courage. When she was down, few people knew it. When others were down, they came to her to be lifted up. I did. I saw her when she was up and I saw her when she was down and I rarely heard her complain. But when she did, it was always with a sense of confidence that things would get better.

Ann was more concerned with others than with herself. Some people learn to use strength only for themselves. Some people learn to use it for other people and for the community. The question is, what and who is their model? The answer so many good people can put forth is Ann.

When she was in the midst of deep personal tragedy, people were amazed to see her reaching out to others. What they could not understand is that Ann knew only one way to do honor unto the dead—that is by what we do for the living. I know that would be her message to us now, that if we remember and honor her, it will be by what we do for the living.

Ann was a true matriarch—for her children, grandchildren, and great grandchildren, of whom she was so proud and with whom she loved to play, travel, cook, or just be. She was also a matriarch for the many people living and dead with whom she was involved—the many, many who felt her influence, as well as the many who never knew her but whose lives were enriched by what she did.

ANN AS FRIEND

Ralph Waldo Emerson wrote, "The only way to have a friend is to be one." Thus Ann had countless friends. A good friend is a treasure, a masterpiece of nature. Ann was my long-time friend. Friendship sometimes lightens burdens. Ann did that for me and for many others.

Ann—yours was a big world. It did not involve just you and your family but also countless others, whom you touched and influenced, who felt your presence.

Ann, I'll miss your wisdom, but I'm wiser because of what I've learned from you. We'll miss your strength but we will all be stronger for having known you.

———

MAX KARL

Memorial Gathering

June 25, 1995

Max Karl died on April 19, 1995. His family mourned, I cried, and friends shed tears. On that day, all of the sons of heaven wept. We mourn his passing and express our sense of loss, but also celebrate his life.

Obituaries have referred to his stature in business and philanthropy. But to me, he was a visionary, a leader, and a man of integrity, generosity, and humility. However, mostly he was my friend.

Max was a benefactor for countless agencies and institutions—he was the single largest individual purchaser of State of Israel Bonds and the single largest giver of funds to the federation's Annual Campaign. As the model and mentor for countless leaders, he was a source of strength.

When you're close to a man, it's difficult to comprehend his great size. Max was a very big man. Maimonides wrote, "The just man is the foundation of the world." Max was a just man. His was a nobility of the spirit. There was a great deal of heaven that hovered over his head. To him, all men were equal. In some societies, people defer to nobility. To Max nobility was the people of learning, of ideals.

MAX AND JUDAISM

The ethical compass of Max's life was his Judaism. He took seriously the admonition from the *Ethics of our Fathers,* "Honor not a man for his possessions; honor him for the right use he makes of them." He went to the synagogue on Yom Kippur and confessed his faults. Yet, I never heard him speak of his virtues.

Max had an insatiable need to help others. The suffering of the Jews in the Holocaust was seared onto his soul. When people cried out, he heard their cries. His sense of peoplehood permeated his flesh, bone, and brain. The Chofetz Chaim wrote, "It is not a challenge to die like a Jew; the true challenge is to live like a Jew." So he lived his faith.

129

Max applied his talents to those efforts that he considered reasons for being. His attitude was expressed to me in the following brief conversation.

When he retired from a very active work life, I, who had retired from a labor of love, told him our situations were analogous, He responded, "Mel, you must not say that. Mine was a business to make money. Yours is a cause."

There were times when I've felt that Max's generosity was misused—that he was taken advantage of by unprincipled people. When I remonstrated with him, he would respond by saying, "Mel, you know I'm an easy mark."

MAX AS PHILANTHROPIST

Max was a great believer in tzedakah. He believed the rich were responsible for helping the poor—that through Tzedakah, we could help make the world a household of love. There is a Jewish adage, "Turn not your face from any poor person and the face of the Holy One will not turn away from you." Max never turned away. Max gave away more money in relation to his means than anyone. Asked why, he answered, "But Mel, I receive more than I give."

There is a Jewish folk saying, "To give a little with a smile is better than giving much with a frown." But Max gave much and always with a smile.

A tireless advocate on behalf of Jewish peoplehood and the State of Israel, Max provided counsel, quietly—almost anonymously—to leaders of the land. His heart was an altar for Israel and the Jewish people.

Aristotle wrote, "Dignity does not consist of possessing honors, but in deserving them." Max was a dignified man.

Some people believe that the object of life is to reach a summit, a high place. As Max saw it, the object was not just in reaching a high peak himself but in helping others move up.

Max never regarded others as lesser than himself. He was respectful of the powerless as well as the powerful, the weak as well as the strong. He pursued the admonition of the prophet Micah: he acted justly, he loved mercy, and he walked humbly with his God.

A man of culture, Max studied the past, lived in the present, and built for the future. To be cultured is not just to read, to understand a painting. It is to understand and sympathize with people. Could there be a more cultured man?

Max always attempted to do more. He took seriously the words of the poet, Robert Browning, "Ah, but a man's reach should exceed his grasp." His reach was great.

Max gave depth to his life by what he did for society, for his community, for the Jewish people, for mankind. In enriching our lives, he enriched his own for he was involved with mankind.

Through my own veil of tears over his death, I know that I'm a stronger person because of his friendship, his goodness, and his kindness.

I wish that I could be confident that I will meet another person like Max, but I'm in the late afternoon of my own life—the wait for a facsimile may be too long. I hope that younger people will some day have the privilege of meeting so noble a soul.

The departure of the righteous diminishes the community. But we're thankful for the blessings of Max's life with us. He leaves behind a legacy of altruism, a guide for people in community, and philanthropic work of goodness and love.

Max, we celebrate your life, and we express our respect for your deeds. You live in our memories.

Ruth Orenstein
August 12, 2005

I've been given the honor of standing here to speak about Ruth. It's difficult, for I grieve. Yet, her example was strengthening enough to help me speak of her, despite the heaviness of heart I feel.

Ruth was a very kind person, and thus, she had countless friends. Every human being is of ineffable worth, Ruth particularly so. She was a leader, a person of great influence. Yet she was modest. She was principled. When others strayed from principle she reminded them of it. She regarded righteousness as the first duty of any individual, come what may. Thus, Ruth had no need to ever use moral blinders. She lived in accordance with the axiom enunciated in Shakespeare's *Hamlet*, "This above all to thine own self be true." She knew of evil as well as good in the world. She pursued the good.

Ruth was a genuine community builder. She helped build a group spirit of togetherness, Kehillah, and community. She was devoted to Israel. She and her Bill spent much time there.

Ruth loved her children and her grandchildren. But the measure of a human being is not just how they treat their own children but also how they reach out to other people's children. The heart as an organ in a human body is small. Ruth's seemed large enough to embrace the world.

She never spoke of her achievements. Ruth had no need for personal recognition. Her need was to help others achieve. She performed countless good deeds, but the greatest of them all was that she caused others also to perform good deeds. Thus, her own mitzvahs were multiplied.

She never regarded others as less than herself. She helped the weak to be strong. There was no deceit in her. She never acted grandly, just graciously. Her dignity did not consist of obtaining honors, but in deserving them. Ruth was always modest, never conceited. She thought of a conceited person not as a sinner, but as a fool. She was rarely angry, but when she was, her anger dissipated quickly.

"Love your neighbor as yourself" is one of the great principles of the

Torah, found in Leviticus. Ruth was true to that principle. She loved people. Her gentle face gave off an aura of love.

There is a Jewish folk saying, "You can wash your hands, but not your conscience." Ruth had no need ever to cleanse her conscience.

When my heart was heavy—I sometimes confided in Ruth—then afterward my heart felt lighter. At times of concern about problems of the community, I would confide in Ruth, and sometimes she would say this and I can hear her now: "Now listen, Melvin," and then I heard a brief lecture—and I felt better. Ruth was a wonderful short-term therapist.

She gave of herself as much as any person. She enriched the lives of many, for she was involved with humankind—whether Jewish, Muslim, Christian, agnostic, atheist, or black or white—for she was a humanist.

The Talmud says, when we appear before the throne of the Lord, He will not ask, "Have you believed in Hashem?" bur rather, "Have you dealt honorably with your fellow human beings?" Judaism, a rational religion, prefers good deeds to pronouncements. It does not call for ritual alone; it calls for righteousness. Ruth was a righteous person.

Sooner or later each of us becomes memories. The best thing a human being can leave behind is a sense of honor and a sense of goodness. Ruth thus leaves us with memories of warmth and love that lift us up and help us bear the loss.

I ask myself why it is that Ruth's passing troubles me so deeply. And I answer, here is an extraordinary woman—extraordinary for a family, great for a community, and a unique friend.

Friendship for many people lasts no longer than the dew on the grass on a morning of a hot summer day. Ruth's loyalty to friends was as permanent as the water in the oceans and the seas. She was the best rare friend of Marlene, Janie, Bert, Allan, and her grandchildren.

Jewish belief places less stress on an afterlife than do most religions; the belief is in a heaven built here on earth, here and now. Now, I hope that somehow Ruth will be getting together with other wonderful women with whom she lived, enjoyed, and worked in this community, who came before her—Ann Agulnick, Esther Cohen, Margaret Miller, Alice Colburn, and others. And of course with Bill: they are planning together to use their collective power to create that heaven—to repair the world through tikkun olam.

We won't in the future see Ruth with our eyes, but she will be with us, as part of us. The past is not dead; it isn't even past.

We may not see Ruth, but we will feel her presence. Her influence and her advice have molded us. Her energy invigorated us.

Her courage strengthened us. We will miss her, but we will be better people for having known her.

Her life was a triumph.

———————

PART IV:
Federation-Synagogue Relations

Federation-Synagogue Connections

Major address to the National Conference of Jewish
Communal Service in San Francisco.

June 1974

Summary

Today, one often hears that there are two major centers of influence in Jewish life: the federation and the synagogue. Yet, some religious bodies and rabbis have spoken of a rivalry between these two and have expressed the fear that, in that competition, the synagogue is losing.

Fast-moving changes in society complicate life for many synagogues. The move to the suburbs, the desire for expensive buildings, the escalating costs of membership and religious school education, as well as additional assessments and capital fund efforts, weigh heavily on people. It has become difficult for many people to regard the synagogue as central, when less than half of American Jews belong to a synagogue and only a small percentage of members actually participate regularly in services.

In a June 1971 publication of the Central Conference of American Rabbis, the seminary of the Reform movement, several rabbis echoed this concern about the future of the synagogue. In particular, one well-known rabbi described the synagogue as having become an appendage of the entrepreneurial capitalistic ethos, controlled by bourgeois businesspeople with rabbis directed to preach their party-line.

Thoughtful federation leaders are perplexed by assertions of competitiveness with the synagogue. The basic mission of the federation is to unify, not to compete, and most community leaders know that well-led synagogues will foster achievement of the goals of the federation. The prevailing belief is in a mutuality of interest.

In an effort to advance cooperation between synagogues and federations, the Council of Jewish Federations and Welfare Funds recently created a task force to study their relationship. It will include consideration of the allocation of federation funds for synagogue-sponsored or related services, including education, chaplaincy, and Kashrut certification.

I believe that federations today are closer to synagogues than ever before. At this National Conference of Jewish Communal Service assembly, we are observant and respectful of religious precepts and practices and are concerning ourselves with the well-being of synagogues, though most of the communal agencies represented here fall under the general rubric of being secular.

We are seeing, more and more, that federations are moving toward the observance of tradition. Sophisticated religious leaders do not cringe when they hear the word secularism, for they know that there is no discord between it and religion. After all, the Jewish Haskalah during the age of enlightenment was a movement that emphasized understanding rather than blind belief. The prime leader of the Jewish enlightenment, Moses Mendelssohn, was a highly religious man whose motive was to strengthen, not weaken, religion by including a focus on worldly matters.

It is odd that representatives of religious movements express the fear that they are losing in a competitive struggle with federations at the very time when federations are moving toward supporting programs for which synagogues have advocated. In many cities, federations now support community chaplaincy programs, but at the same time discourage those community chaplains from officiating at funerals and weddings, lest anyone view such activity as being competitive with the synagogue. Federations now observe Kashrut at community events to enable participation of observant people. Many federations today provide consultation, formally or informally, to synagogues on their building fund efforts and financial problems, which was unheard of 15 or 20 years ago. Federations now include among their responsibilities the funding of day schools and large-scale programs of education.

I live in a community in which many major federation leaders are synagogue members, officers, presidents, and the like. All agencies that have come into being in recent years, including overnight and day camps, homes for the elderly, and nursing homes, family and children's agencies, and the federation itself, observe Kashrut as a matter of course, and the Jewish Community Center operates a full-scale kosher dining facility. The protestations of a decade ago that the observance of Kashrut in community-operated agencies and in community events represents an imposition of the will of a minority on the majority have faded away.

The federation-sponsored chaplaincy program reaches out to the affiliated and unaffiliated alike and works closely with the Council of Rabbis, which the federation had a role in organizing eighteen years ago. A Brith Millah program is supported by the federation. The Orthodox-oriented day school was the first in the United States to be supported by a federation on a deficit basis (i.e., in precisely the same ways as communal agencies are supported).

It's a complex time for Jews. Everyone seems to have his own definition as to who is and what is a Jew, and this may continue for a long time to come. We appear unique to other religious groups that abide by relatively uniform definitions. There is something special about a people who can live without uniformity, with so much diversity, but yet in unity. After all, for some Judaism is a religion, and only a religion; for others it is peoplehood. For some, it is an ethnicity, and for still others it is all inclusive.

In 1965, *Look Magazine* printed a famous article entitled "The Vanishing American Jew," questioning whether Judaism and the Jewish people would survive. But the Jew has not vanished, though *Look Magazine* has. One thing is certain and that is the strong sense of kinship among Jews. The cries of Jews in the Soviet Union are heard in Israel. The tragedies experienced by Jews in Israel move us to tears in America. The murder of twenty children in an elementary school in Ma'alot, Israel, just a few weeks ago, brought mourning to Jews in San Francisco, New York, and elsewhere.

No Jew is really alone for each shares a common sense of history, destiny, and identity with the other.

Some long nostalgically for the days when the synagogue was the focal point of Jewish communal activity, when it served the sick, owned cemeteries, and cared for the poor. Today, the synagogue is essentially a house of worship, a membership organization, accountable only to its members, though with a special relationship to a national body to which it may belong. Synagogues meet individual and family needs—providing educational services for children, social activities for adults, and personal and group counseling on religious matters. Some rabbis provide counseling and guidance focused on social and emotional problems as well.

THE FEDERATION AS THE MODERN KEHILLAH

Since the turn of the 20th century, the federation concept has developed and grown ever stronger. It is a transcendent continuation of the Kehillah created by government edicts in many countries of Europe centuries ago. Jews were required to contribute to the Kehillah in accordance with their means. That was a form of an enforced tax through which the Kehillah, representing the community, supported the synagogue and carried out communal responsibilities—providing education for children, hiring religious personnel to officiate at rites of passage and other religious ceremonies, and giving assistance for people who needed it because of economic want or sickness.

The federation, through its agencies, is a continuation of the Kehillah in voluntary form. Through the federation, people work collectively to deal with common concerns. They do so as consumers of service, contributors of money, and as an army of participants in fundraising campaigns. They have a presence in the thousands as directors and advocates of and for federation-affiliated agencies in communities in which they live throughout America. Continental and international agencies, such as the United Jewish Appeal, the Jewish Agency for Israel, and others with substantial name recognition, are partners of the federation. But federations have become the primary organizations through which Jewish people collectively help to sustain Israel, a rallying issue for Jews for 2,000 years of dispersion until and since the rebirth of the Jewish State.

With the passage of time, federation priorities and functions change, and synagogue and federation concerns have converged. Federation support for Jewish education and cultural services has increased. Federation-related boards of Jewish education provide support services and sometimes funds for synagogue sponsored schools.

An aftermath of the Holocaust is the ever more profound concern with the protection of Jewish life and the survival of the Jews as a people. The birth of Israel made security of the state a precious priority. The Jewish faith calls upon people to make a heaven for humankind on Earth, here and now, and not to wait for the afterlife. Federation and synagogue both call for acts of tzedakah and of lovingkindness. People who spend time in prayer, but who do not commit acts of tzedakah, forsake the belief for which the synagogue as an institution stands. If we pray in the synagogue for freedom for Soviet Jews, how can we not support the federation that finances the work done to obtain that freedom? Is it not a contradiction to pray in the synagogue for a "next year in Jerusalem" if the words are not followed by supporting the federation? Simply put, federations are instruments for the application of much of synagogue teaching, for putting into practice much that the synagogue and prayer advocate. The aims of the synagogue—improvement of the lot of humankind and the world through Tikkun Olam—are to a great degree given meaning through Jewish agencies and institutions, which with federation encouragement, support, and organization, provide services that improve the quality of Jewish life and enhance Jewish identity.

SYNAGOGUE-FEDERATION RELATIONS

In recent years, synagogues have requested financial support from federations to fund some synagogue-sponsored services, such as education for children, continuing education for adults, new counseling services, and youth activities. Often, these requests are made without any mechanisms in place to ensure accountability for the quality of services provided or the ways in which the funds are actually spent. In many communities, programs and services are sponsored by both the synagogues and the communal agencies. For example, the federation may fund Jewish education in community schools, and synagogues provide their own religious schools, to which the federation and boards of Jewish education relate and sometimes support financially. Both synagogues and the JCCs sponsor cultural programs; both synagogues and community relations agencies offer programs and events to promote interfaith, interracial, and interethnic understanding and engage in social action.

By and large, synagogues do their work individually and rarely in cooperation with other synagogues. Likewise, the coordination between synagogues and federations in conducting programs remains scant, and available data indicate that by and large relationships between them are shallow. It is almost as if the federation operates as the secular state from which the synagogue is detached. But total separation of the synagogue and federation from each other makes little sense in a world in which there is a growing convergence in interests.

In some places, pulpit rabbis, by virtue of their roles, hold membership on federation boards of directors. Some serve in prime positions including that of president or of campaign chairman. However, other rabbis consider communal work, in addition to synagogue responsibilities, to be a burden. Federations should give careful thought to board membership and select members only on the basis of their interests and demonstrated willingness and capacity to serve, thereby relieving such uninterested rabbis from their communal responsibility.

Several years ago, the United Jewish Appeal embarked on the 100% plan. This was a call upon synagogues to encourage their members to give, without reference to the size or quality of such gifts. It is logical to expect members of synagogues to be in the forefront of giving, as they put into action the call of religious doctrine. It is significant therefore that the United Jewish Appeal would even think it necessary to create the 100% plan. Unfortunately, there is no indication that the appeal resulted in any significant increase in the amount of funds raised, although some synagogues and rabbis did wholeheartedly involve themselves in the critical fundraising effort during the October 1973

Yom Kippur War when Israel was in such great peril.

On a personal note, I was saddened when, during the early part of that critical fundraising effort, one rabbi in my community took it upon himself to conduct his own campaign for funds for Israel through his synagogue. Unfortunately, he was obtaining gifts in modest amounts, in the hundreds of dollars, from people from whom federation campaign workers would have requested thousands. In a telephone conversation I demanded a halt to this effort, to which the rabbi had no choice but to agree. I believe my shout was loud enough for him to hear in his synagogue miles away, without benefit of telephone. This experience in 1973 was a repetition of another during the 1967 Six Day War in which another rabbi behaved similarly. In these instances, two rabbis grasped opportunities for personal notice and the marketing of themselves. In speaking of this conduct to a highly respected rabbi and confidant, he commented to me, "Mel you must remember that before he was a rabbi, he was a man."

Any lack of cooperation between the synagogue and federation contradicts the purposes for which they stand. The federation plans, creates, and sustains services for the elderly, for youth, and for Jewish education and culture. It provides for the homeless in Israel, helps people living in harsh conditions in places where they are not welcome, and aids in their emigration from lands in which they cannot live as Jews. It helps provide opportunity for free choice—whether to make Aliyah to Israel or to immigrate to the United States or to other lands open to them. Funds raised often make life possible where it would otherwise not be. Are these not things for which the synagogue stands?

In the future we will see new forms of support for synagogue-sponsored schools. Such support will be on the basis of financial formulae determined jointly by synagogues, boards of Jewish education, and federations. It will be provided by federations in their determination to upgrade Jewish education, wherever it exists, including synagogue schools. There are questions about how such joint work will be carried out, because after all, the synagogue has traditionally been the business only of its members to whom its services were available. Synagogues may open their schools to children of non-members, and there may be some participation by the federation in determining the conduct and reviewing the quality of synagogue-provided educational programs. The result will be new forms of synagogue-federation association.

CONCLUSION

Federations have never and do not now view the synagogue as a rival. We look to it as a partner and must be prepared to work cooperatively with it. But federations cannot be cash registers alone for synagogues, just meeting their fiscal needs. There will need to be some joint planning of services. This may require adjustments on the part of the synagogue; they will need to be open to federation review of portions of its program, as occurs with communal agencies. Federations will have to exercise considerable care and discretion in such cooperative work.

I believe the time is imminent when synagogues and federations will work more closely together to achieve common objectives of both. When this occurs, a new chapter in Jewish community life will unfold and the precious work of both the synagogue and the federation will, more effectively than ever, be done.

The New Tabernacle: Dedication and Celebration

Address given at the dedication and celebration of the
Beth El Ner Tamid Synagogue.
February 1984

Some people may be surprised that I, a federation executive, am the speaker at this wonderful synagogue dedication. Some remember the differences we have had and even the imagined differences. Should we not learn to submerge them and to emphasize the mutuality of our hopes? In loving relationships, lovers quarrel and then they make up. There is a joy in making up. We have experienced that joy for we are part of one family, one mishpacha.

How easily we misunderstand others. I learned about these misunderstandings early in my career in this community. When I was fresh out of the Army and serving as the new assistant director of the federation, I attended my first meeting of a group of people who wanted to organize a Jewish convalescent home. The meeting was held in an Orthodox synagogue, Beth Israel. When I was called to speak, there were mutterings in the room—"Oy a Goy, a Deutsch." I was taken aback. I knew so little of such distinctions. I was born in Poland; but what if I was a Deutsch? That was in 1946, just after the Holocaust, when we had just picked up the bones of our brothers, flesh of our flesh. And so I proceeded to give my talk to the group in the language that it understood best—Yiddish, the language of my childhood. And they were shocked. Even then, though, there were differences of opinion about the place of Yiddish in Jewish life, and there were those who objected to the idea of Hebrew as the national language for the State of Israel for which we prayed and struggled.

There are always differences in a family, but there are things that we hold in common. After all, this synagogue is a tenant of the Jewish Educational and Cultural Complex building with the federation as its landlord. Those of you who are aware of the relationship know that it is good to rent from the federation. Who ever heard of a landlord concerned that the rent charged be very modest, so that the tenant will have sufficient money to furnish and maintain its building? But then, who ever heard of a tenant so considerate of a landlord?

BUILDING THE TABERNACLE

It is a fitting time to celebrate the building of a temple, the contemporary form of the tabernacle. For just last week we read the Torah portion in which God commanded Moses to see to it that the tabernacle would be built. In the Torah, God says to the people, "Bring me gifts from every person—of gold, silver, and copper—blue, purple, and crimson yarn, fine linen—lapis—other stones." For God's dwelling had to be a suitable sanctuary; it could not be like other places. You have built a new Beth El— a new house of God. It is also written that those who come to the sanctuary, to the Beth El, the house of God must be pure and ready to conduct themselves with dignity as a holy people.

Beth El is an old synagogue that has been in several locations but that carries on the traditions. We Jews have never been particularly concerned with space and, in truth, have been the most transient people in history. After all, Jews were resident in North Africa from the time of the Romans and now hardly live there at all. And so your synagogue moves into a new location that we never thought of occupying a generation ago.

When God commanded the building of the tabernacle, he meant *the* tabernacle. Now, there are many synagogues as there are many groups in a community; we try to bind groups together to care for each other. Rabbi Akiva said that the greatest principle of Judaism is to "love your neighbor as yourself." That requires that this synagogue be strong as an institution of Judaism and then that it join with other institutions, uniting together to make one Jewish community. Each synagogue is maintained by a voluntary membership, but each is united with the Knesset, the congregation of Israel, by our common heritage of faith and duty.

The sanctuary that you have built is a place to which observant people come to remind themselves of what God wants of them: deeds of loving kindness and of tzedakah, as well as observance of law, study, and prayer.

In most ways, the federation for which I work, and which is yours as well as mine, is an extension of the synagogue. Its mission is to carry out the deeds of lovingkindness that God calls for. Remember that our religion is one that has always preferred action to talking about it, good deeds instead of pronouncements. As in the words of Micah, "to do justly and to love mercy and to walk humbly with thy God." The Jewish community is built on the principle that every individual is of unlimited worth and that each Jew is dependent upon the other.

Life in the American Jewish community is different now than in the days of the ghetto, which forced Jewish togetherness as a result of intolerance and tyranny. In the ghetto, the Jewish community could carry on all of its social and religious life in narrow confines. There, because of the overt hostility on the part of the prevailing majority, whether it was under the cross in Christian countries or under the crescent in Moslem lands, we created services and activities for ourselves for we were prohibited from sharing in the institutions of others.

Now, in free societies, we build into our agencies and institutions meaningful Jewish values and an appreciation of our cultural heritage. In the final analysis, our proud community structures would collapse unless they are built on a foundation of committed Jews responding to a compelling spiritual mandate. For example, if Jewish Community Centers would be simply places that separate the Jewish children from other children, but do not provide programs with Jewish components, or if Jewish social service agencies provided wonderful services and care for the well-being of people, but nothing uniquely Jewish, then we would question what makes these agencies Jewish.

A word about money. The federation, with which I and you work, raises money. Money was needed to build this new synagogue. People gave of themselves kindly as God called upon them to do. When God called for the building of this tabernacle, He called for people to give in accordance with

147

their means. It was the quality of what they gave, not the quantity, that determined their own purity and their own equality of partnership. Dignity must also be preserved for those who receive. That is how we do it in a good community and a good federation. We learn also to honor those who give of their means. We learn to understand the admonition in the ethics of our fathers, "Honor not a man for his possessions; honor him for the right use he makes of them."

Thus, your contribution for the creation of a new Beth El is a contribution not only to yourselves but also to those around you and those who will follow you.

RELIGION – PRAYER – NEEDS

Our Judaism differs from other religions in that it is concerned not only with the salvation of the soul in the afterlife but also with the hallowing of life in the here and now and for the sanctifying of human conduct in society. Our ethical and spiritual influence has been universal. What others call religion today, any religion, is in essence a spiritual crystallization of the collective experience of the early Jews.

Clearly, we cannot survive as a people if our heritage and our principles are not taught diligently to our children. And so the synagogue and organized Jewish community have worked together for centuries. In the 15th-century kingdom of Castile, Spain, each community, to support Jewish education, was required to institute special levies on kosher meat, wine, inheritances, and the celebration of weddings. Any community that consisted of forty or more households was required to hire and pay a teacher to teach Talmud. Carrying on this tradition, before this community had adequate Hebrew schools, this synagogue had a vibrant school that was open to the whole community, non-members as well as members. It entered into a partnership with the community to finance the service. This synagogue is among the few in America to have been in such a relationship.

The federation and this synagogue are both concerned with the perfection of society as well as the salvation of the soul. Our institutions are intertwined. In the words of Jeremiah, "Seek the welfare of the community in which you live and pray for it, for its welfare will be your peace."

There is a talmudic principle that goes, "Man should perform very righteous deeds, even if he does so only for ulterior motives, because he may thus learn to do the right for its own sake." The federation calls upon people to do righteous deeds. I would prefer that their motives be pure. That is where the synagogue comes in, because it teaches people the basis for deeds of lovingkindness—tzedakah, not charity.

The synagogue and federation pursue common objectives. To put it simply, the federation is an instrument to put into practice what the synagogue teaches. It brings together the entire community, all as one, to organize and implement the programs that give meaning to what the synagogue stands for. We build a voluntary community based on the thesis that unity is possible without creating uniformity.

We preach in the federation that it is possible for people to work together, despite their differences. How uninteresting life would be if everyone felt and acted the same. If there were no differences to spur our thoughts, life would be very monotonous. What we need to do is accommodate ourselves to differences and to freely express our opinions at the same time as we emphasize things we hold in common and that are so dear to us.

Many Jews, here and elsewhere, identify with other Jews only out of a sense of rejection by the prevailing forces in society. This identification comes from a feeling of not belonging. That kind of identity is dangerous and is viable only when the outside pressures of anti-Semitism are strong. It means that when we are not kicked, we will fall apart.

Twenty years ago, one of the favorite questions of the Jewish agenda was whether we would continue to exist as a people if there was no anti-Semitism. Would we become like all other people in the world? Would we assimilate completely and become homogenized into other societies? We answered through the synagogue and the federation that it was the Jewish people who created the idea of monotheism, the idea of brotherhood and of living together in unity as well as diversity. We remain a Jewish people able to tolerate all kinds of differences and yet maintain a basic sense of concern and identification with each other, a people able to create and maintain a culture even in the face of persecution, and a people concerned with religion on behalf of the individual and not the use of the individual on behalf of religion. That kind of people does not die.

Some of our institutions long ago became enamored of the term "non-sectarian." It was almost as though we, as Jewish people, could obtain acceptance only if we could tell people that our agencies were created not for ourselves, not to give meaning to Jewish life, but rather to ingratiate and curry favor of others. And the magic word "non-sectarian" became part of the vocabulary of American Jewry, proclaiming to the world that Jews are not parochial and not self-centered.

In the past American Jews have too often done the following:

- neglected Jewish survival
- emphasized integration of the Jews into the general American scene
- devoted ourselves to bringing Jews into the mainstream, erasing the special qualities that made us different
- concentrated on acceptance by others instead of acceptance of ourselves
- neglected that which made us distinctive.

Today, the Jewish community is getting stronger. Although there are times when, I confess, I thought we would be farther along, we are moving along, all of us together.

One lesson we have learned better than other Jewish communities is that we need to stand together. There are times when no one else but ourselves will save us. That makes us ask ourselves the question, "How deep is our love?" How much do we care for the survival of the Jewish people? When we have burdens cast upon us, will we carry them together?

None of us knows what the future will bring. Fifty years ago, we did not expect the decimation of much of European Jewry. A hundred years ago, we did not dream that in the United States there would arise the largest Jewish community in history, and we did not predict the re-creation of the State of Israel. Thirty years ago, in Milwaukee, there were two neighborhoods in which Jews lived: the East Side and the West side. Who would then have dreamed of a Beth El synagogue in Mequon?The quarrels of a generation ago are no more. We have learned more about living together and working together, about planning together, about saving lives together, and about using our money to enrich life. Those of you who have used your money to build this new synagogue have enriched yourselves. After all, what value is money if it is not used to enrich life?

Yet, you, who lead this synagogue, and you and all others who lead the Jewish federation and the community, have not yet done enough. There is so much to do. Our mission is plain. Our task is clear: as you build this synagogue you must also build the community. Our mission is to work collectively with all the Jewish people, to go forth as one Jewish people, to pursue the dreams of our fathers and forefathers, and to inspire our young so that they will realize them.

PART V:
The Urban Crisis and the Jewish Community

The Negro Revolt

Remarks to the Milwaukee Jewish Welfare Fund Board of Directors.
September 1963

It's Erev Yom Kippur, a time for reflection, for thought, for determination, and for soul reaching—a good time to think about the most precious of all our possessions: freedom.

OUR COUNTRY IN CRISIS

The United States is living through one of the great crises of its history, and there is turmoil among us. The question is raised as to whether the problems of the Negro, of 20 million downtrodden people, are our problems. The answer must be yes, that they are the problems that must be addressed by every human being, by every American, and most urgently, by every Jew.

There are those who believe sincerely that Jews must be in the forefront of this struggle so they can obtain the favor of the Negro; they fear that the Jew will inevitably be marked by the Negro as the usurer, the rent gouger. However, the welfare of the Negro is important for Jews for far greater reasons, because we are the people who say and believe that we are our brothers' keepers. Much that is decent on this Earth, such as the concept of tzedakah, of justice, righteousness, and decency of people toward people, is rooted in Jewish tradition and thought.

Some Jews require a reminder that whereas the Negroes were slaves, the Jews were as well, and some have forgotten the six million who perished in the Holocaust. Some people refuse to look upon horror and to do anything about it, just as the world looked away when Jews were dying. Most Germans pretended that the problem was not theirs. A new play, "The Deputy," recently opened in Switzerland. It avers that the late Pope Pius XII failed to take a strong stand against the Nazi genocide of Jews and that he was thus, in part, responsible for the slaughter of European Jewry. The same play under the title "The Representative" is playing in other European countries. Commenting about the play, Dr. Albert Schweitzer said in a recent published statement that not only the Catholic Church but also the Protestant Church were "guilty."

Dr. Schweitzer continued, "We are all guilty today for the reason that we were guilty then. The Catholic Church bears the greater guilt, because as a great international organization, it could have taken some action, but the Protestant Church, too, was guilty of simple acceptance of the fearful inhumanity of the persecution of Jews." The question for Americans, and especially for Jews who have suffered so much, is whether they, as a group, are guilty of the acceptance of the oppression of Negroes.

A few days ago, sixty U.S. Senators joined in a resolution condemning the Soviet Union for discrimination against Jews. They appealed to the Soviet Union "in the name of decency and humanity" to cease executing persons for alleged economic offenses, and they asked the Soviet government to fully permit freedom of religion for Jews and all others within its borders. These are our Jews. They are you, and they are us. If we are concerned with them and demand that others be concerned, how can we ignore problems of people in our midst?

THE NEGRO DEMAND

What has happened in our country? Demands of an underprivileged, undereducated, underfed, ill-housed group of 20 million reached the ears of the people, and the U.S. government passed laws, and these laws called for equality, and they were flaunted by bigoted people. And so the 20 million, that large minority, decided that the time had come to achieve freedom, and they intensified their struggle of more than 100 years. With it has come a passionate demand for freedom that will inure to the benefit of all people. This impatient cry for equal rights is expressed in every art form by Negroes and whites alike; as in Bob Dylan's folk song, "Blowin' in The Wind."

How many roads must a man walk down
Before you call him a man

How many times can a man turn his head
and pretend he just doesn't see

The answer, my friend, is blowin' in the wind
The answer is blowin' in the wind.

THE NEED TO ACT

We as Jews are a people who have experienced the most glorious achievements, and we have suffered the most horrible tragedies. For people like us there can be no complacency.

The struggle for freedom and for human values goes on all about us. The battle against humiliation and poverty is renewed. Our obligation is to act. Our Jewish tradition teaches us that indifference to people in trouble is a sin. Callousness toward the suffering of others and neglecting opportunities to help people are sins. Jewish tradition also teaches, as Herzl said when he dreamt of a Jewish state, "If you will it, it is no dream." We Jews have always believed that good things can happen only if we make them happen.

Our Jewish community is given dignity not only by what it does to rescue Jews from oppression wherever in the world they face it, by the kind of Israel we help to make possible, and by the kind of Jewish community we help to develop here at home but also by the kind of America we help mold, and I suggest we help mold it now. Proclamations of concern are given meaning only through a demonstrated compassion, by what we actually do, not only for our own aged, our own handicapped, and our own refugees but also by what we do for other people.

A COURSE OF ACTION

We must recognize that those who ride the civil rights bandwagon, drawn by a Negro leadership, have all sorts of motivations. Pious declarations without action constitute words without substance. Thus, I would suggest that we make this meeting a first step through which we, as a community, join with other decent, humane forces working on behalf of dignity for all people, regardless of the color of their skins.

We within the Jewish community must examine our own conduct to be certain that it is exemplary. We have reason to expect it is in most instances, but we must verify and satisfy ourselves that it is. I propose that our agencies follow this course of action:

1. **Employment Practices**: Much that is done by Jewish agencies requires Jewish professionals, but in those instances in which it is the practice of organizations to employ non-Jews, there should be certainty that those non-Jews be hired regardless of race.

2. **Admission Policies**: If any agency has found it suitable to serve non-Jews, as is the case with hospitals and Jewish Vocational Services, it must examine its practices to determine that there is no discrimination against any groups because of race.

3. **Business Dealings**: All agencies, to the extent possible, should avoid business dealings with suppliers who are known to discriminate against members of minority groups. It should be noted in this connection that the Catholic Archdiocese in Chicago and other groups, religious and secular, have taken action along these lines and that the federal government requires evidence of non-discrimination from business concerns with which it deals today. A procedure should be developed whereby Jewish organizations proceed along similar lines.

4. **Coalition Building**: The Milwaukee Jewish Welfare Fund, as the central instrument of this Jewish community, should join with the Milwaukee Jewish Council in convening a meeting of representatives of every communal, health, and welfare agency to discuss the actions described above so that each may be aided in examination of its own program— all of this to conclude with a public declaration on the part of the Jewish community with regard to its practices.

5. **Volunteer Leadership Involvement**: Several hundred people who are members of the boards of directors of the agencies of this community in turn employ thousands of others. Many of our leaders own and operate real estate companies. Such people are in a position, because of their own

identification with welfare agencies and human values, to take the lead in demonstrating their concern for others. It is recommended that means be found to encourage such people to employ people and to sell housing without discrimination in recognition of the fact that the Negroes' struggle is for freedom, education, *housing*, and *jobs*. The federation should bring together groups of real estate operators and employers to educate and to influence them in connection with the rental and sales of real estate as well as employment practices.

6. **Education:** It is recognized that securing better jobs, better housing, and social advancement requires educational opportunity. The Welfare Fund staff has been studying the question of education for the deprived and noting the basic importance of special educational opportunities in preparing deprived children for freedom and opportunity. It suggests that such thoughts and material available be shared with the Welfare Fund's Committee on Group Services as a step in the direction of encouraging appropriate public and private bodies to improve educational opportunities.

Jews who are altogether familiar with the humiliation of being unable to sleep where they wish to sleep, who were quarantined in ghettos for so many years and who still are in many places, who were denied opportunities in all sorts of employment and still are in some places within our country, who were unable until the end of World War II to practice medicine in many hospitals and still cannot, who entered many universities on a quota system and still do, who cannot join many social clubs, including some within our own city, and who have met hate and murder can hardly be onlookers when one of the great battles for freedom goes on before their eyes. Our history, our collective experience, our tragedies, and our glories as a people dictate that we have a special stake and responsibility in all of this.

In the face of oppression and brutality, let us not be silent.

The United States: A Troubled Nation

Presented at the General Assembly in Atlanta.
November 1968

_____

DIMENSIONS OF THE PROBLEM

We are living in a period of more divisiveness within our country than at any time since the Civil War. The Prime Minister of Canada recently expressed concern over a possible revolution in the United States, cautioning that such a revolution could spill over into Canada as well as Mexico. His warning evokes thoughts of the unstable conditions and frequent revolutions found in our neighbors to the south in Latin and South America.

In the last few years, we have experienced shocking violence in America —expressed most dramatically by the assassinations of national leaders. Much but not all of this violence is race related. When our popular president, John F. Kennedy (JFK), the youngest person to be elected to the presidency and the first Roman Catholic, was assassinated in 1963, he was in the process of aligning himself with black leaders in a drive for civil rights spurred by savage attacks on black people by government officials, as well as by racist groups in the South. JFK had proposed legislation that evolved into the Civil Rights Act of 1964, combating race discrimination in employment, access to public accommodations, voting literacy requirements, education, and the like.

Martin Luther King, Jr., the most respected black leader in America, was assassinated on April 4, 1968. Using the Mahatma Gandhi strategy of non-violent resistance, King was helping bring about progressive social change in America. He had led major demonstrations for civil rights and equal opportunity in

Birmingham, Selma, and Montgomery, Alabama. He had been a force for passage of the landmark Civil Rights Act of 1964, proposed by JFK.

Opposing the more militant approach being advocated by other black leaders, King had asserted that the world was not "going to respect the United States—if she deprives men and women of their basic rights of life because of the color of their skins." His "I Have a Dream" speech, given in front of the Lincoln Memorial in Washington D.C. during the 1963 March on Washington, will reverberate for years to come. His was the pinnacle of leadership among the black population of the United States, a model of inspiration for people of all races. One hopes that his example will inspire a new sense of self-respect for American blacks and enhance their eagerness to achieve progress without violence.

King's death came less then a year after the riots in American cities in the summer of 1967, which left in their wake many dead and injured, countless burnt-out buildings, and thousands of arrests. His death, combined with the events of the terrible summer of 1967, prompted President Johnson's formation of the National Advisory Committee on Civil Disorders, chaired by Otto Kerner Jr., the Governor of Illinois. This committee found the riots to be a result of black frustration and lack of economic opportunity. The report stated, "Our nation is moving towards two societies, one black, one white—separate and unequal."

On the heels of King's death came the assassination of Robert F. Kennedy on June 6, 1968. A trusted presidential advisor for his brother JFK and, at the point of his death a U.S. Senator from New York, Robert Kennedy was in the process of realizing his aggressive vision for civil freedom and justice, and he was the leading candidate for the Democratic nomination for the presidency. He had begun work on projects to help poverty-stricken Negroes in New York, advocating a forceful agenda to eliminate discrimination on all levels. A champion of the disadvantaged and a supporter of the integration of all public facilities and the Voting Rights Act of 1965, he may well become an icon of American liberalism. With the death of the younger Kennedy, America has been shaken yet again and has even more violence to overcome.

The well-known British philosopher, Arnold Toynbee, predicts that the tenure of the United States as a great power will be briefer than that of any other great power in history. The same Toynbee, however, described the Jews as a "fossilized civilization"—and I do not believe him on either count.

Our country is torn by dissension, disillusionment of our youth, conflict over war, and more overt opposition to the nation's policies than we have known for a century. Young people openly burn their draft cards, some riot in our streets, and many rebel against repressive police policies and power, all symbolic manifestations of a troubled country. It is no longer our country right or wrong—disenchanted people feel free to say that it can be wrong. This is a time when tensions easily flare up, groups set against groups, and a racist, George Wallace, is not only a candidate for the presidency of the United States on the ballot of every state but has also received the votes of one of every seven voters. The urban crisis affects all of America, for ours is an urbanized society. We look into the face of catastrophe in this great land of hope and promise in which so many promises are unkept.

The issue before America is freedom versus disappointment, freedom versus discontentment, freedom versus suffering. In recent years, an underprivileged, undereducated, underfed, ill-housed minority of 20,000,000 people have demanded equality. The impatient cry for equal rights is expressed in every art form by black people and white alike, as in the folk song, "Blowin' in the Wind":

How many roads must a man walk down, before you call him a man?

How many times must a man turn his head and pretend he just doesn't see?

The answer, my friend, is blowin' in the wind;

The answer is blowin' in the wind."

A liberal America takes up the cry, grasps the black man's hand and says, "We will overcome.

INTEGRATION VERSUS SEPARATISM

Black people may be created equal in body, but they are unequal in opportunity. Fourteen years after the great Supreme Court decision mandating school integration, schools still remain segregated, and those attended by

161

black children remain inferior. Expenditures for instruction in segregated public, elementary, and secondary schools are far lower for black students than for white pupils.

Black people pressed for integration, but their demands were ignored. Rejected by white society in schools, neighborhoods, and workplaces, some have reacted with a new demand for separatism—for control of their own institutions. That agitated cry comes from people who feel forsaken by the vast majority of Americans. It comes out of the past, the hundreds of years of oppression, the unimplemented integration, and the impatient wait for equality. Black people clamor for black power. Some see in the idea of distinct and separate institutions a hope for a sense of equality, although the idea itself is born out of a feeling of hopelessness.

The pluralistic society of the United States is often described as a "melting pot," and many people fear the move toward separatism. However, complete separatism will never exist in our country. Certainly, our society would be unwilling to grant to the black population any portion of the country, neither the state of California nor the state of Iowa. And even if America was willing to create so incredible an enclave, it would not succeed any more than did Biro-Bijan in the Soviet Union for the Jews. However, a sense of influence and power can help black people build bridges with white society and achieve improved mutual respect.

Some people sensitive to the massive problem of the black population are making sincere efforts to provide them with (1) jobs so that people can have money with which to support their families, (2) suitable housing, and (3) improved education so that this vast underclass will have greater opportunity. But has enough been done? There remain large masses of unemployed blacks. The movement away from dreadful housing is minimal, slums have been expanding, and there has been little progress in the field of education. Considering the vastness of the problem, the impatience of the black population, the alienation, and the enmity, the public response has been minimal

Many white people who are deeply concerned with problems of humankind, who are humanists seeking an improved America, identify with the plight of this large minority of people and are attempting to help them. When they do, however, they often find black people hostile and unwilling to accept some of the jobs available to them.

We need to understand the reaction of large numbers of blacks who are in a rebellious mood. They sense that, although many white people feel a sense of compassion, it is not strong enough to have brought about significant change. Black people understand that the compassion of white people is often overshadowed by fear, and this understanding results in greater disillusionment, disorder in the streets of our cities, unrest, and a spirit of disruption. The seeds of virtual insurgency were planted by those in power years ago, and now we are harvesting an extraordinary crop of bitter frustration and hate. If we do not plant new seeds of understanding, provide more work opportunities, and move quickly toward better housing and improved education, then our society may indeed reap the whirlwind.

HISTORIC PARALLELS AND VARIANCES IN JEWISH AND BLACK HISTORY

Our own Jewish history has been dominated by pain. Edward H. Flannery*, an outstanding Catholic priest, writes of 23 centuries of persecution of the Jews—history's longest hatred, which began long before the Common Era in Hellenistic and Roman times and then intensified under Christianity. The Nazi genocide, the Nuremburg trials, the Eichmann trial, and attention given to anti-Semitism by the Second Vatican Council have focused attention on anti-Semitism and xenophobia.

A question about the status of blacks that is raised frequently by some Jewish people is, "We made it—why can't they?" We must remember that we Jews came to this country as a fearful lot and on sufferance—our emigration was made possible by an order of the directors of the Dutch West India Company to Peter Stuyvesant, the domineering Director General of New Netherland, to permit a group of 23 Jews fleeing the inquisition in Brazil to live in the Dutch colony, "provided the poor among them shall not become a burden—but be supported by their own nation." We took care of our own,

---

* The Anguish of the Jews (1964) by Edwar H. Flannery

because we were ordered to, as well as by choice. Jews faced severe restrictions in housing, business, education, and employment in America. We responded by learning how to become entrepreneurs and professionals, and we began to make it economically. Fathers and mothers deprived themselves; promising that it would be better for their children.

In the more than 300 years of settlement in America, we never dreamed of using force to gain what we needed; we often felt insecure. We lived with deep anxiety as we looked at what was happening to our brethren in other parts of the world. Sometimes we curried favor with dominant forces. We created agencies to protect ourselves from those who would demean us and deprive us of rights. We became more secure and advanced more readily through cooperation and alliances with other groups.

Black people came to America under completely different circumstances. Whereas Jews paid for their passage to come to America, in search of freedom and independence, blacks were transported in chains from Africa and elsewhere to slavery in America as human chattel in the commercial slave trade. They were, in effect, property, belonging to owners—their masters. The anti-slavery movement culminating in the abolition of slavery during the Civil War was the greatest human rights crusade in American history.

Yet blacks remained essentially enslaved. They fought in American wars, but only in segregated units. Black revolutions swept the world, with nearly all of Africa becoming free. Undereducated and untrained black people in Africa took their land back from the British, the French, Spanish, Portuguese, and Dutch, who centuries earlier had created colonial empires. Heartened by the movement of their black brothers, celebrating the victories of Supreme Court decisions in recent times, and legislation in America that said they were equal, blacks, hoping for freedom of opportunity, pushed aside those described as "Uncle Toms" and declared they would no longer tolerate obstructions in their path. They looked upon laws that kept them separate and unequal, declared them to be unjust barriers to progress and vowed not to abide by them, and then there was suppression. The blacks' response to this suppression has often been peaceful and nonviolent, but most recently feelings of deprivation and anger have brought violence of a kind that Martin Luther King had discouraged.

Can we understand this violent response? We Jews have been the victims of unjust laws that at various times in our history fostered persecution and even the murder of Jews. Such laws, in their most extreme form, permitted the slaughter of six million of our people. Was not the defense put forth by Adolf Eichmann that he obeyed the law? When laws are unjust, when they promulgate unequal education and opportunity, and suffering, and when they create a siege of discontent, should we expect people to abide by them?

There are vast differences between the historical experience of Jews and blacks in America. We, a fearful minority, felt that we had everything to gain through the evolutionary process. Because we knew we had no other haven, we were too fearful to be impatient. In contrast, the black people are impatient. Moreover, they have power in numbers: 20 million is a much stronger force than 5 million. Although black people may suffer in other parts of the world, they are attempting to seize political power in those places.

NEGRO-JEWISH TENSIONS

It is a bitter historical tragedy that there should be tensions between blacks and Jews, both of whom have experienced so much suffering. How ironic that these two groups should be turned against each other, when both would become victims of a strong reactionary movement in America. Some Jews need to be reminded that they were slaves, just as blacks were. The Negro spiritual, "Go Down Moses," after all retells the events of the Bible in which God commands Moses to demand the release of the Jews from bondage in Egypt:

When Israel was in Egypt's land, Let my people go.

Go down Moses, way down in Egypt's land.

Tell old Pharaoh, let my people go.

Experienced black leaders understand Jewish concerns. Whitney Young, director of the National Urban League, had this to say at last year's General Assembly

I feel strongly that the Jewish community has an extra-special obligation in the area of civil rights. I believe that for two reasons; (1) I believe that there is no community that knows better what hate can do. There's no community that has suffered the impact of bigotry for so long and hatred for such illogical and irrational reasons. (2) I also believe it because I think the Jewish community actually knows that the Negro may well be the first line of defense. If the Klan gets past us, the John Birch Society gets past us, and the White Citizen's Council, but more important, if this whole crop of people who suddenly have middle class incomes but are not undergirded with comparable cultural or educational backgrounds, this new group of affluent peasants, the ones that live in the Bronxvilles and Ciceros of our society, if they succeed in doing away with him—you know who is the next line of defense.

But our identification with the suffering of the large black minority stems from our concept of tzedakah or social justice; our heritage demands that we do not separate ourselves from the community. Recently, black leaders have used the moral precepts of Hillel as a civil rights slogan: "If I am not for myself, who will be?," to which of course we add "If I am not for others, what am I?"

Jewish people have had and continue to have a significant leadership presence in black organizations. Jews have been board members and the heads of the Legal Defense Fund of the Urban League and of the National Association for the Advancement of Colored People (NAACP); the NAACP's current president is Jewish.

The memories of the Holocaust—six million strong—are seared onto Jewish souls. Yet the black man sometimes faces a ghetto merchant, fair or unfair, looks upon him as an exploiter, and that becomes his image of the Jew. We are concerned when the word "exploiter" becomes synonymous in the black person's mind with the word "Jew," just as Jews were marked as Shylocks when Shakespeare created that blemished image in his Merchant of Venice. How strange for Jews to be so regarded by the black who has inherited the ghetto, which is still defined in many dictionaries as an area in which Jews reside, restricted in activity, and where they do, in fact, still live in some places or in the counterpart of the ghetto, the melah of many Muslim lands.

BRINGING FORTH PROGRESS

Responsibility for bringing about progress for black Americans belongs to all Americans and requires employing without discrimination, reversing discrimination, making up for years of injustice, developing suitable housing and appropriate health and welfare programs, and adapting the educational system to the needs of children from homes of culturally deprived parents. There is the urgent need to develop a larger, stronger class of black business-people and professionals, who can work collectively with decision makers within the broader society.

However, I fear that a good share of what is being done today comes under the general rubric of currying favor. Black people may well perceive that we act out of a sense of guilt. It would be better to use our energies to help motivate humanist forces in an effort large and strong enough to deal with a crisis crucial to all America.

Let me illustrate: The University of Wisconsin Medical School, in the comparatively progressive state in which I live, graduated a black physician for the very first time a year ago in 1967; America's largest Jesuit Catholic university, Marquette, in Milwaukee, has very few black students in attendance on scholarships. We could well stimulate a total community effort so that universities no longer practice discrimination but instead provide special opportunities for black students. We can be of the greatest service for black people by using our efforts as catalysts so that America acts.

It will take a long time for society to make progress, to bring to reality the words of the song, "We shall overcome." It has taken centuries to produce the deprivation, the suffering that has given rise to this crisis in America. An intense ongoing struggle by large strong forces is required to diminish the problem and to bring about justice for the black masses of our land and equanimity in our cities.

THE JEWISH RESPONSE

As Jews we identify with the struggle of black people for freedom. When our six million perished, the civilized world looked on, and most people who witnessed the horror pretended not to see. For oppressed people, the cruelty of the oppressor is hateful—the silence of the bystander insufferable.

Our Jewish tradition teaches us that indifference to people in trouble is sin. Callousness towards the suffering of others, neglecting opportunities to help people—that's sin. To us civil rights is not just a Negro cause; it is a human cause. We Jews have always believed that good things could happen only if we make them happen. As Theodore Herzl said when he dreamt of a Jewish state, "If you will it, it is no legend." We feel a special obligation to act . But the question is how to act, and I am convinced that many of the answers that have been put forth, even by well-intentioned people in the Jewish community, are not the correct ones.

In response to demands for equality, Jews and Jewish organizations ask what they can do. Some Jewish community relations agencies have created black-Jewish dialogues in an attempt to achieve understanding. In doing so, some unwittingly implied not just a special Jewish concern, but a commitment to help beyond the capacity of the Jewish community, itself facing so many problems. Many of us live in cities in which our number represents 1 or 2 or 3% of the total population, a small trickle in the flood of humanity. Yet, we have a strength that is disproportionate to our number that flows from the concept of community, togetherness, through the Jewish federation and Welfare Fund idea. Bulletins sent out by the Council of Jewish Federations publicize the work of Jewish communities in helping improve the plight of black people. We read of hospitals serving black people, of Jewish vocational services providing some guidance and aid in job finding, and of Jewish camps and community services for Negroes.

However, we cannot alone alter the fabric of the total society—to deal with the root causes of poverty, inadequate education, unemployment, and poor housing requires the involvement of the whole society. Whatever we do alone as a people cannot be enough; it would only dilute what we do for ourselves and would fail to alter the plight of our black neighbors. These efforts could appear to be a promise that we would then be unable to keep, resulting in frustration and resentment.

Which Jewish community feels sanguine about its capacity to provide all the necessary resources to meet Jewish needs—at home and abroad—needs for which only the Jewish community will provide? Only the Jewish community will sustain agencies of Jewish life—Jewish schools, Jewish community centers, services for college youth and teenagers, Jewish family services, etc. If we were to attempt to shift major resources to help blacks, we would merely endanger the services that make possible Jewish survival and yet fail to meet the needs of the black community. We do belong in the struggle, but not as a public relations venture or out of fear that the tide of power will shift in the direction of blacks in whose good graces we must remain, but because we are in truth their ally and the ally of all suppressed people.

Some Jews have suggested Jewish fundraising on behalf of the Negro community. We should ask ourselves what the results of that fundraising would be? How much money could we raise? Would we have a campaign on behalf of black people in place of an Israel Emergency Fund? Would we dilute our support for Jewish community relations agencies that work to improve understanding between blacks and Jews? It would be well that we understand our own limitations. It is foolishness for Jewish people to believe that we can alone alter the tides of history.

We need to recognize that we can do little alone and that we can be more helpful if we are operative as part of the whole community thrust. No community has had more experience than we. We are a people with a genius for organization that can be used to catalyze the total community into action. The primary mission of the Jewish federation is community organization: to assess the needs for service, determine their costs, create budgets that represent programs in dollar terms, market human needs, and organize fundraising efforts to meet Jewish needs everywhere. We can use this communal strength on behalf of others, through community coalitions so that the public is mobilized to lash out against oppression.

These facts should be clear:

1. The urban crisis is a matter of huge importance, requiring the work of all of American society.

2. It cannot be effectively dealt with by fragmented approaches and a proliferation of individual projects.

3. Many organizations address themselves to the problem as much out of a need to look good and seem relevant as out of a confidence that they will truly ameliorate the problems of people.

4. The Jewish community by itself can do too little to materially affect the situation, and careless and unwise efforts could suggest Jews have a special sense of guilt, rather than deep concern, resulting in charges of tokenism. The Jewish community would be placed between the white community and the black in an untenable no man's land in which we could be damned by bigoted whites for what we do and by black people for not doing enough.

Here are the components of an elementary action program in which the Jewish community could take part.

- **Legislation**—The Jewish community can help in the struggle for justice and equality, by advocating progressive legislation that reverses discrimination by influencing our government to practice discrimination in reverse as is done in Israel—obtaining special consideration for black people in education and employment, for example. It can, with the rest of society, advocate for increased opportunity that makes amends for hundreds of years of discrimination. We are largely a suburban people, and the battle for the city can be won in the suburb. We can help the suburban Members of Congress understand that their suburban constituents seek improvement in the whole society.

- **Movement by the Voluntary Sector**—We can help form coalitions that bring together constructive forces to obtain social change. The mission of such coalitions should be to move in all fields—housing, jobs, education, and the environment—planfully and with all possible resources.

- **Health and Social Welfare**—As we move to help catalyze the whole of society into action, we may use our strength to provide advice and to help fill some gaps in services, until the day when government assumes greater responsibility for the well-being of all people, supplemented by efforts by the private sector.

- **Urban Crisis Funds**—National United Way publicity material contains calls for each individual United Way to give priority concern to problems of the inner city. But has there been movement in this direction? All that we have seen is a shifting of small amounts of money from traditional agencies to other organizations in the inner city—too little to have real meaning to the inner city and enough only to weaken the traditional partner agencies of the United Ways. This shift is happening in many cities all over America, and with it could come the denigration of the United Way idea.

- **Helping Organizations That Serve the Black Community**—If United Ways do not grasp the opportunity, there should be consideration to the development of United Negro Funds. This development could be shaped to some degree by Jewish community experience. Black people and groups would join together as did Jews almost one hundred years ago, raising money and meeting needs that have been collectively determined. In such an effort, the black community would need to submerge internal differences by concentrating on common concerns. Such efforts would enhance feelings of self-respect. The outcome can be a greater sense of equality and a respect between black and white communities.

Jewish federations may be a special help in the development of central black community organizations. With their unequaled know-how on community organization, the federations can advise and guide without substantially diminishing attention to Jewish services and Jewish funds. Any diminution in attention to Jewish communal responsibilities should be avoided for that could increase Jewish suffering without benefiting anyone.

CONCLUSION

The struggle for freedom and equality can only be conducted effectively through a unity of purpose on the part of influential groups and people throughout America. Only then can we reduce anger and diminish riots, destruction, and harm to America. Our role can be to pique the conscience of America and, in consort with other groups in the private sector, to move forward with programs that can help the black community organize for self-help purposes. We should do things not for black people but with them, helping them build independence and not dependence.

We the Jewish people cannot be onlookers as a great battle for freedom goes on before our eyes. We must be part of the struggle. We may engage in limited well-focused programs to help tide things over a bit. But this must be a very big effort; to help the black and the poor is to change America—and that is, save America.

PART VI:

Retirement: Continuing a Meaningful Life

PRE-RETIREMENT PLANNING:
PSYCHOLOGICAL AND LIFESTYLE ASPECTS

Seminar given as chair of the Committee on Retirement for the Association for Jewish Community Organization Professionals (AJCOP) in New York.

May 1997

Retirement, a rite of passage, is of importance to every professional in the field of Jewish community organization, as well as our spouses, children, and family members with whom our lives are intertwined. Years ago, retirement would have been merely a brief period between departure from full-time work to life's end. With today's increased life expectancy, we need to focus on our emotional and psychological well-being during the longer and longer periods of retirement.

In 1900, life expectancy for men in the United States was 44, and for women, it was 49. By 1974, life expectancy for men had increased to 68 and to 76 for women and has gone up gradually ever since. The proportion of people in the United States over age 65 was just 2.5% in 1850, 4 5% in 1900, and 12% in 1985. The percentage of elderly has been growing twice as quickly as the rest of the population during the last 30 years. The number of the elderly is expected to grow from 29 million now to 64 million by the year 2030. That means many more retirees and many more senior professionals.

Retirement can be either a time of loss or of freedom. Good things come with retirement—diminished pressure, fewer fevered debates, a quieter telephone, and the freedom to use time as one pleases. But along with the good comes the bad—a loss of status and a reduced sense of one's importance, erosion of work-related friendships, a feeling of being excluded and even faceless, and a fear of encroaching enfeeblement. Retirement can be a challenge that one rises up to meet or an intimidating threat.

With careful planning, we can achieve in retirement the ideal espoused by the Roman statesman, Marcus Tullius Cicero, 2,100 years ago: "The thing that is most outstanding and chiefly to be desired by all healthy, good and well off persons is leisure with honor."

ATTITUDES TOWARD SUCCESS, WORK, AND AGING

We live in an age of diminishing idealism, when private gain is accorded much higher value than public service. Our times preach that money means success. Our altruistic profession sometimes moves away from its kindly liberal character to an identity with pragmatic, political, competitive values of the business for-profit world. Executives of necessity wear several mantles. One was fashioned when some of us were young—the humanist, Jewish, and community-oriented mantle. Another mantle is tailored by the management function, in keeping with being an employer as well as an employee.

A field committed to people and community that was characterized initially by kindness sometimes treats committed people with a harshness reflective of big business in which people—labor—simply constitute the largest cost factor. Such attitudes militate against adequate health insurance and pension programs. Cost of living adjustments in pensions are few in number, an unfortunate omission that it is hoped will be corrected in the future.

Those of us with a spark of humanism, whether we are new to the field, seasoned retirees, or executives who after all have the greatest power and responsibility, should strive to liberalize such benefits. Good executives in good Jewish communities and agencies are people, by and large, of high quality from whom we should expect dignified conduct. As Aristotle wrote, "Dignity does not consist of possessing honors but in deserving them."

Americans regard age as an enemy; society is prejudiced against the elderly, contradicting the prayer emblazoned on so many facilities for the elderly, "Cast me not off in my old age." It was not always so. Historically,

Jews respected the elderly. (Deuteronomy 11:13 & 21) states, "Ye shall hearken diligently unto my commandment that your days may be multiplied and the days of your children in the land which the lord swore unto your fathers to give them as the days of Heaven upon the earth." A long life was regarded as a supreme reward for virtue.

Similarly, in ancient China, sons had to obey their fathers and younger brothers their older siblings. The authority of the patriarch increased with age. People actually pretended to be older than they were in order to be treated deferentially. In China, each generation succeeds the predecessor one. In contrast, in the United States, each generation supplants its predecessor.

Attitudes toward work have varied from society to society and have changed through the centuries. In Hellenistic times, the Greeks considered working for a living as ignoble. In contrast, the Jewish attitude was always that work adds to human dignity—that through work, a person is raised above the level of the animal. Rabbi Eliezer (ca. 100) said, "Work is to be cherished, for of all the creatures that God created in his world, he gave work only to man."

Sociological studies demonstrate that work sharpens one's alertness and awareness, expands one's horizons, and increases a person's sense of self-worth and self-respect. In an interview in January, 1990, Katherine Hepburn said sagely, "Work never hurt anybody but lack of it can destroy people."

RETIREMENT—A NEW CONCEPT

Until passage of the Social Security Act in 1935, most Americans worked until they died or were forced by illness to quit. Before the 1930s, only the railroad industry had a retirement program, and it came into being not because older people were no longer skilled but as a way in to enable senior workers to give way to the young.

Corporate pension programs followed the development of Social Security, developing slowly and proliferating during a fifteen-year period from 1965 to 1980. Unions pressed for Social Security and retirement programs for two reasons: (1) to reduce unemployment among the young by retiring the old and

(2) to improve the financial status of the elderly. The rallying cries of the business and industrial world were "room at the top" and "new blood." In 1950, 46% of men over the age of 65 worked. By 1970, that number had diminished to 25%. The emphasis was on youth.

The Social Security system established the age for retirement at 65. President Roosevelt and his cabinet debated what the age of retirement should be and then decided to base it on the German system established under Otto von Bismarck in 1872. But the average life expectancy in Germany then was in the forties, and hardly anyone lived to the age of 65.

What a silly age for retirement is 65. How irrelevant it is to the capacities of people today and to today's life expectancy. Granted, people in their sixties and seventies are less able to climb mountains, and the surgeon's fingers may lose dexterity. But their minds are no less facile; their knowledge and understanding of people as individuals or in groups and of the nature of community is at a high level, and their capacities continue to grow. Invention, as Jonathan Swift wrote, "is the talent of youth but judgment is the talent of experience and age."

Some of the greatest contributions to humankind came from people far older than 65. Golda Meir became Prime Minister of Israel at the age of 71. Goethe wrote Faust when he was 84. Pablo Picasso produced some of his most famous paintings when he was between 85 and 90. Frank Lloyd Wright completed the New York Guggenheim Museum at the age of 89. George Bernard Shaw broke his leg when he was in his late seventies by falling out of a tree. Georgia O'Keeffe did some of her most notable work when she was in her nineties, and she was not the only nonagenarian of distinction. In Jewish communal service, these people would all have been in retirement.

People grow old at different times in life. The night of one person's life may be the early afternoon of another's. I know people who in their nineties are pleasantly young and people at age 40 who are unpleasantly old. But then, what is old? When I was 10 years old, 25 seemed old; at 30, I was told that life begins at 40; at 50, I spoke of the past as being prologue; at 60, I was old enough to know how little I knew. But one thing I am certain I do know: retirement at 65 is ridiculous.

PLAN FOR RETIREMENT—DO IT EARLY

Just about everyone should plan for retirement long in advance. In her book, New Passages, Gail Sheehy illustrates that need by citing the experiences of two men, former Presidents George H.W. Bush and Jimmy Carter. Each resisted retirement, but was forced into it by their employers— the electorate. Each thought it happened too early and was unprepared, but for different reasons.

Carter did not anticipate his election loss. Shattered, he had to give up his living quarters in the White House. He was near ruin financially, had debts of $1 million, and faced bankruptcy and even the loss of his farm and his house in Plains, Georgia. In an interview given shortly after leaving the presidency, he said he faced "a potentially empty life." Soon, however, he adjusted to retirement. He made money by writing books and devoted himself to Habitat for Humanity as a volunteer. But he missed world affairs. Nine years later, he awakened with a start in the middle of the night with an idea about making better use of his time and recapturing a sense of worthwhileness. He brought his ideas to President Bush and was then given a more active role in foreign affairs than any former president, with assignments in Panama, Ethiopia, Nicaragua, Somalia, and Haiti.

George H. W. Bush was equally unprepared for retirement. He could not believe he would not have a second term as president. He had no place to live, as his house in Maine was not winterized and his residence in Houston was just a hotel suite that he maintained for political convenience. He owned a vacant lot in a Houston suburb, but no house. He took his family on cruises, went fishing, and jetted around the world from golf course to golf course. But he became bored, depressed, and befuddled about what to do with his life. Mrs. Bush, better prepared, wrote her autobiography and a book about the family dog and campaigned for literacy.

We are not presidents of the United States, but we all face psychological, emotional, and financial problems as did Carter and Bush. Often, we feel a loss of identity, of worthwhileness, of work-related friendships, and of financial security. When we define our work as a cause and feel our destinies intertwined with the Jewish community, retirement can be devastating. In our profession, we create programs to help people plan how to live their lives. Is it not ironic that we've neglected to plan for ourselves!

The field of Jewish communal service has recognized the need for retirement planning. In 1983, a paper entitled "A Proposal for a Bill of Rights for Retirees" appeared in a publication of the National Conference of Jewish Social Welfare. It called for more than a pension plan. It recommended medical insurance, financial and psychological counseling, continued suitable work, opportunities to wear out instead of rusting out, involvement in national meetings like the General Assembly, and roles for retirees as volunteers on boards and committees. Those proposals were germane then and remain so today.

THE CORNELL UNIVERSITY STUDY

Cornell University recently completed an intensive study of retirement using a sample of about 800 people in upstate New York in all levels of work, from factory jobs to CEOs. It found post-retirement life expectancy to average about 30 years and that the average person retired early because of a wish to escape from routine, boring work. Phyllis Moen, the lead professor in that study, funded with an initial grant of $2 million, expresses the views of her colleagues as well as her own with a sardonic comment on 30 years of retirement, "That's an awful lot of golf." One man in his eighties commented, "If I'd expected to live this long, I would have figured on doing something besides playing golf."

That study strongly indicates that people need and want their lives to be more purposeful—the happiest are those retirees who do some form of work. The Cornell study cites social isolation, a feeling of rolelessness, and a hastening of the onset of poor health as common risks in retirement.

AJCOP STUDIES ON RETIREMENT

The Committee on Retirement of AJCOP, which I chair, has completed two significant studies on retirement, one in 1988 and an update in 1995. The 1988 study found that comparatively few Jewish communal professionals retained their jobs after the age of 65. A fairly substantial number did work after retirement, but outside the Jewish community, rather than within it. Of those who worked in a Jewish agency, it was only infrequently the federation. In short, in 1988 our retirees were conspicuously absent from community organization volunteer roles in federations and agencies.

The 1995 study found that the situation had changed. Possibly, because of the work of AJCOP, increasing numbers of retirees were involved in federation work—in community planning, public relations, marketing, leadership development, grant applications, computer programming, cash collections, maintaining archives, and teaching students.

Executives had begun to see in retirees an untapped resource and created conditions that facilitated their involvement in decision-making and campaign roles and as part-time workers.

As part of the 1995 study, ACJOP surveyed executives of large federations. A majority of the fifty-four executives who responded indicated that had a suitable program existed, they would have (1) employed retirees on a part-time or temporary basis; (2) regarded their deployment as volunteers as credible, sensible, and wise; and (3) been thoroughly supportive of pre-retirement planning programs.

COMPONENTS OF PRE-RETIREMENT PLANNING

Pre-retirement planning must begin when people are relatively young—it is not postponable, if for no other reason than the financial one. A dollar put aside at the age of 40, 45, or 50 has far greater worth than one saved at the age of 60.

Any decent program of pre-retirement planning will include these components:

- work for those who wish it and are suitable for it
- activity as volunteers
- pre-retirement planning and counseling, individually and in groups

Such planning, illogically absent from our own field, exists commonly now among major companies. For example, Chrysler Corporation, in cooperation with the United Auto Workers, sponsors a program in which I participated as an observer and from which I learned. It includes financial planning, medical insurance and services, estate planning, legal planning of wills and trusts, housing, work opportunities, ongoing education, and lifestyle planning.

PROFESSIONAL TO VOLUNTEER

Retirees constitute a considerable source of skilled volunteers for the Jewish community, for federations, and for agencies of all kinds. Most are very honorable, idealistic people. Honor has no time limit; ideals do not age.

Some years ago, I met with the Committee on Personnel of CJF. I noted with interest that every person present was past retirement age if they had been staff members of federations. CJF's readiness to have retired professionals join them was strong and clear. We need to establish a similar suitable climate in our communities and agencies. Executives have major responsibility for creating this receptivity to using retired professionals as volunteers.

DECIDING WHERE TO LIVE AFTER RETIREMENT

When deciding where to retire, generally retirees consider four alternatives: moving to the Sunbelt, moving to where the children live, returning to their hometowns, or remaining in place. This decision requires careful thought.

Many people love the Sunbelt. However, they may love it in winter but hate the heat in summer. The newsletters published by retiree and seasoned citizen organizations contain countless stories of people who move to the Sunbelt because they had reveled in vacations there but found they could not live there year round and often return home. Many people are unhappy with retirement areas in Florida, Arizona, and California because of those communities' homogeneity. Most people want contact with people of all ages.

The state with the highest concentration of older people (over 60) is Florida, but the draw of the Sunbelt is diminishing. The states with the greatest proportion of people over 60—after Florida—are surprisingly Arkansas, Iowa, Kansas, Nebraska, Missouri, South Dakota, and Oklahoma. Areas that have become popular with retirees are the Midwest, the Carolinas, and college towns, particularly for well-educated people who prefer high culture to warm climate and seek out lectures, concerts/theater, and continuing education. Other areas that are attracting retirees are Upper Michigan, northern California, the Ozarks in Arkansas, and the Poconos of Pennsylvania.

Before making the decision where to live, retirees should think carefully about these issues:

- Don't be quick to give up the snow for the Sunbelt without really trying it out, not just once but in various parts of the year.

- Moving to where the kids are may be a great idea; but you may move only to see your child transferred by his company shortly afterward and you are left alone in a strange place.

- Nostalgic memories may influence a person's decision to move to the place in which he or she grew up, but nostalgia may blur reality. Communities change, old landmarks may be gone, and old friends may no longer be there. It could be like moving to a strange city. It may be that you really "can't go home again."

- Studies by the AARP find that 83 percent of retirees want to remain in their current homes. This, of course, includes poor elderly who cannot afford to move and people tied to the land in rural areas.

What Is Home?

Home is many things—it is psychological as well as physical space, and it is an extension of one's personality, where there are familiar possessions, familiar landmarks, and friends. If you leave it, you may miss the sense of self built up over the years and your involvement with other people. Moreover, our children and grandchildren often regard our homes as their second homes.

However, one must consider some important issues when one chooses not to move. A big house can make one "house poor" and can drain one's energy. An apartment may cost less, allowing the freedom to travel and visit the kids. Inevitably, some of us will require different kinds of living arrangements—some forms of assisted living, congregate care, life care communities and, when absolutely necessary, nursing homes.

HEALTH AND HEALTH CARE

Two of the greatest concerns of older people are their financial security and their health. The health of older people has actually been improving in recent years, because older people are taking better care of themselves. Many older people take aspirin daily to prevent strokes, heart attacks, and certain forms of cancer. Women take estrogen supplements to prevent osteoporosis and heart attacks. The future is expected to bring an annual drop of 1.5% in the prevalence of disability among the elderly. This improvement has already occurred; for example, Duke University studies have found that the number of people over the age of 65 who are unable to bathe or dress themselves has diminished from 25% in 1982 to 21% in 1994 with the favorable trend continuing.

When I see my doctor, I'm conditioned to hear two words—exercise and diet. And so, I exercise and sometimes diet, for I have learned that exercise and diet can help reverse the negative effects of aging, not just in the 60s but in the 70s, 80s, 90s, and beyond. Exercise, join a gym, or purchase suitable exercise equipment and use it at home. Walk, swim, stretch—exercise of all kinds contributes to one's physical and emotional well-being. It is true that if you don't use it, you'll lose it. Follow simple rules like drinking less alcohol and more water, reducing fat and carbohydrates, and increasing fiber intake.

HEALTH INSURANCE

All of us need to be well insured. We need to learn to monitor and understand insurance programs. Policies supplementary to Medicare benefits are absolutely essential. What we cannot afford is inadequate coverage.

Most communities and agencies do not extend medical and health insurance to retirees, although such coverage is called for in the personnel standards of the Jewish Communal Service Association. If professionals on all levels and organizations including AJCOP and CJF all work together, health insurance for retirees will become a standard benefit.

DEVELOPING INTERESTS

It would be well for all of us to develop interests outside of work. Some of our colleagues have developed interests in carpentry and cabinet making.

Gardening is a great challenge. It is one of the most satisfying hobbies around because with it comes a sense of achievement. Some people are reading about and studying subjects that have always interested them. I have learned more in retirement about Jewish life than I ever knew in my work life.

When retirees are asked what they will do when retired, common answers are play golf, go fishing, or travel. People of financial means set out eagerly on six-month trips around the world and are initially enamored by what they see. They travel for a time, but soon disenchantment sets in; they become homesick and cut their trip short. No one can travel all of the time. Fishing, golf, beach walking, and television all have their place. Experience finds, though, that they become a bore if that's all there is.

Much can be done in retirement, including professional work and volunteer work. We need a climate that makes both possible and meaningful. There is more time available for family, for children and grandchildren. There is time for work in jobs we choose to work in, not just for pay and time to help other professionals.

This is a question for any retired individual: "Is there a future in the future?" When Mordecai Kaplan was asked what he would do when he retired, he said he would "put four new tires on the car and go full speed ahead." That's the way it ought to be for us in retirement—full speed ahead working on worthwhile things we choose to do and sharing leisure with those we love.

The mission in life, as I see it, is not just happiness but worthwhileness. For us in this profession, who define our work as a cause, our mission should include making it possible for every person in our field to enjoy the last third of life in happiness with worthwhileness.

We know now from these studies that many of our professionals want to work after retirement and that many agencies can deploy them gainfully and effectively, most commonly on a part-time basis. We know that a suitable system is required to match work and worker, and we have set about to create this system. Through the combined labors of AJCOP, the CJF, federations and other pertinent organizations, we should succeed.

FROM GENERATION TO GENERATION: DISCORD AND HARMONY AMONG YOUNG, VETERAN, AND RETIRED PROFESSIONALS

Presented to the National Conference of Jewish Communal Service
in Concord, New York.

May 1987

This paper reports on the preliminary findings of a study on retirement of professionals in Jewish communal service. It was carried out by the Committee on Retirement of the Association for Jewish Community Organization Personnel (AJCOP). It synthesizes the opinions of older professionals who responded to a survey questionnaire and reports on the views expressed by federation executives. The questionnaire was supplemented by many interviews with retirees and with younger, active professionals, mostly executives of federations. I have, of course, added my own impressions and views.

To young people who may feel that retirement is an issue that does not affect them, I would reply by noting that not only will it affect them in the future but it also affects them now. Attitudes we manifest toward professionals who are 70 mold our attitudes toward professionals aged 30 or 40.

Of course attitudes toward aging are shaped by the culture in which we live. In today's society in which we emphasize so much that is shallow, culture has a short shelf-life. I find that today's teens do not know very much about Shakespeare or Keats or Byron, but they do know about the movie box office hero of the moment. They may know who the president of the United States is, but will be unable to identify Winston Churchill.

Yet our work in the Jewish community is intergenerational. It depends not only on the present but also on the past; it requires that the experience of each generation be known to the ones that follow and that it should be respected, not only because we wish to avoid the errors of the past but also because it is good to learn from what our predecessors have done. We do not live in the past, but the past continues to live in us. A wise man draws from the past, lives in the present, and works for the future. Although true history seldom repeats itself in precisely the same way or form, it reveals lessons that we would be well advised not to ignore.

The number of older people in developed countries continues to increase, and our nation's population is graying. In the United States, people over 65 represented 2.5% of the population in 1850, 4.1% in 1900, and grew to 12% in 1985. It grew twice as quickly as the rest of the population in the past 20 years. The number is now approximately 29 million and the U.S. Census Bureau projects an increase to 64 million by the year 2030. There will be many, many older people including professionals amongst us.

We say in our work that the elderly represent a priority concern. Homes for the aged emblazon on their walls and stationery, "cast me not off in my old age." Sometimes we treat it as though it were a slogan rather than a hope or a prayer. But any decent program for the elderly includes opportunities to work, not only for the poor but also for people of means. Yet we, in Jewish communal service, hardly do such things for ourselves.

ATTITUDES TOWARD AGING

Societies differ in how they regard and treat the elderly. In ancient China, respect increased with age, and people pretended to be older than they were just so they could receive such deference. Confucius (ca. 500 BCE) wrote, "At 15 I applied myself to the study of wisdom; at 30 I grew stronger in it; at 40 I no longer had doubts; at 60 there was nothing on earth that could shake me; at 70 I could follow the dictates of my heart without disobeying the moral law." To this day, the elderly are treated with great respect in China.

Older people were treated differently in Europe. In the Middle Ages, property was conquered by the sword, and physical strength was seen as the highest value. The Renaissance exalted physical beauty and rejected the aged who were regarded as ugly.

We Jews though have always been known for the respect with which we have treated the elderly. In Deuteronomy God says, "Ye shall hearken diligently unto my commandment that your days may be multiplied, and the days of your children in the land which the lord swore unto your Fathers, to give them as the days of heaven upon the earth." (Deut 11:13 & 21) It also says in Deuteronomy that "if a son refuses to obey his father and all attempts to make him yield are in vain, then the father must take him before the elders of the town. . . . All of the men of his city shall stone him with stones that he die." We looked upon old age as a supreme award for virtue as it is written in Proverbs, "The fear of the Lord prolongs days but the years of the wicked shall be shortened." (Leviticus 19:32) adds, "You shall rise before the aged and show deference to the old."

Unfortunately, the modern American Jewish community does not seem to operate according to those biblical precepts. How often do we really follow the commandment, "Honor thy father and mother"? Admission to some homes for the elderly is determined by economics, not by the needs of the senior. Financial interests, including availability of government reimbursement, often fosters placement in nursing homes, rather than the development of preferable alternative forms of care that would keep the elderly person in the community.

END OF IDEALISM?

In Jewish life we need to ask ourselves whether we are living by Jewish values or are adopting societal mores just to fit in. The 1980s are a time of sharp contrast from the cooperative spirit of the years following World War II. Today's culture is enamored of materialism and get-rich-quick schemes, in which private gain is accorded a much greater value than public service. Idealism is on the wane, weakening the idea of community as a cooperative enterprise and conflicting with the spirit of collegiality and cooperation. Corporations, government, and even religious bodies are tarnished by scandal. Competitive tendencies become more dominant than an altruistic concern for our fellow humans, our colleagues, and our community. Our times teach that because money equals success, accumulating wealth is therefore the primary goal. Fortunately society and our Jewish communities include people of strong conscience, who use their means not only for their own comfort, but to aid their fellow men, and for improvement of society.

Given the society in which we live, what should we professionals strive to be? The answer to that question is idealists, people who chose this field because we are concerned about the strength of the Jewish community. Yet we are affected by the business world in which the search is so often for personality, not character. Some among us, who counsel on decision making ourselves, pursue competitive rather than altruistic motivations that are characteristic of the impulses of the majority of us and the generous people who voluntarily give of their means and their time.

Our survey and interviews with older professionals and retirees reveal that they are no less affected than younger professionals by the society in which we live:

- Some expressed bitterness because their pensions were not large enough to maintain their lifestyle.

- There was a substantial correlation between financial resources and the feeling of well-being, with some people reporting considerable assets beyond what they could have accumulated during their working lives alone.

- A substantial number of those who do work after retirement do so outside of the Jewish community, and they cite several factors for this, including a lack of available work in the Jewish community and the preference for the slower pace and reduced stress of work found in the non-Jewish sector.

- Some are involved in voluntary activity within the Jewish community, but at least as many or more are involved in the general community.

RETIREES—A VALUABLE RESOURCE

What is especially noteworthy is that very few who had worked in Jewish federations are involved after retirement as voluntary workers or leaders within the Jewish community. Except for a very few who were in positions of very senior status in New York, they are conspicuously absent from involvement with national Jewish organizations.

Retirees, with the exception of those who retain part-time positions such as endowment fund directors, almost never attend the General Assembly of the Council of Jewish Federations, the largest and most significant of all leadership meetings. They are not involved with, or by the UJA, and almost none attend the meetings of the Jewish Agency for Israel. Although the cost of involvement on national and international levels may be a discouraging factor, the fact that even those who are well off economically are absent from such activity suggests that the real reason is the failure of communities to ask them to be involved.

Volunteers who are asked to participate in community affairs are presumably selected with great care and thought by presidents, officers, and others, who of course, look to professionals for guidance and recommendations. A considerable number of retired executives feel that their successors are uncomfortable with their presence and prefer that the retiree be of little consequence.

And it is true that when the retired professional is not involved and does not read or keep in touch, in time his or her capacity to be useful does diminish. Of all the self-fulfilling prophecies in our culture, the assumption that aging means decline and poor health is probably the deadliest. Although research has demonstrated there are many ways to age, we set the aged up for senility and death when we draw them away from meaningful work. We isolate the elderly in our profession when we exclude them from our activities or deliver a message that there is no longer any role for them. This isolation is aggravated when many retired people spend their last years in sunny, childless ghettos, away from children and grandchildren as though they are waiting to die.

The failure to recruit good volunteers from among retired professionals contradicts our stated concerns with keeping people active and useful. Unlike some retired professionals who cannot continue in their fields because of physical changes—for instance, the surgeon whose hands have lost dexterity—the retired Jewish communal professional does not rust: Physical tiredness is generally not an issue. Committed people get less rather than more tired. If older people do get tired, why is it that so many of our most important lay leaders are in their seventies and eighties. Is it a fact that professionals get tired but that big givers do not?

Of course, the wish to remain active within the community is not universal. Some professionals regarded their work as drudgery or boredom, and they celebrated their freedom on the day they quit. Then there are those who lived their work, who never learned to leave it at the office because it was not a job, but rather a way of life. To such committed people, retirement that brings with it complete separation from that which they loved is like drinking hemlock.

Retirees in other fields may feel similar pangs of separation, but they are felt more keenly by those in an endeavor like ours. Jewish communal service is predicated upon an understanding of each other, a sense of fellowship, and a feeling of membership in an enlarged family—the Jewish people—whose members care for each other. For some retired professionals, crossing the bridge from staff positions to retiree is a form of human destruction.

RELATIONSHIPS BETWEEN ACTIVE AND RETIRED PROFESSIONALS

Federation executives expressed a wide variety of attitudes toward older professionals in their midst, who often were their direct predecessors. Feelings ranged from comfort with them; to appreciation of their predecessors as sources of information about the past, counsel, and advice; to outright rejection.

Many executives feel discomfort when their predecessors are around. This pertains also to other fields of endeavor. A recent study on university presidents and their predecessors was done by the Association of Governing Boards of Universities and Colleges. It found a commonplace discomfort on the part of presidents with the very existence of predecessors who were high achievers and had warm personal relationships with people with whom the new president must now interact. *

---

* "The Many Lives of Academic Presidents: Time, Place, and Character" (1986) by Clark Kerr, former President of the University of California.

A few federation executives held attitudes toward their predecessors and other senior professionals in their midst that were refreshing, constructive models. They welcomed them as professionals of long standing who had amassed knowledge and influence to be passed on to their successors. Unfortunately, most professionals had little knowledge of professionals of past generations. Although they knew about professionals of very recent vintage, particularly those, of course, with whom they had worked, these federation executives were unfamiliar with the names of professionals of just a generation ago.

Some executives manage situations so that people with whom they personally are uncomfortable are not selected for decision-making roles. When this occurs, it deprives the community of participation by people with varied points of view, required for consensus building. The same stratagems may be deployed in keeping retirees from active roles in any significant lay capacity. Absence of such veteran professionals is often read as disinterest. People may become disillusioned when they see a retired professional, whom they thought was committed, leave the scene; they may see the retired professional's conduct as making a mockery of his or her prior commitments. It inevitably denigrates the image of professionals in general.

Now, obviously, the Committee on Retirees and I believe in continuing careers for retirees in part-time work or as voluntary leaders as well as professionals. They do, after all, retire—they are not even necessarily very old. Great thinkers have much to say about aging. Three hundred years ago, Jonathan Swift wrote, "Every man desires to live long but no one would be old." Bernard Baruch, a prime advisor to Franklin D. Roosevelt, wrote, "To me, old age is always 15 years older than I am." He was 85 when he said that for the first time. When the great baseball pitcher, Satchel Paige, moved from the Negro to the Major Leagues and people pressed him for information about his age, he would answer, "How old would you be if you did not know how old you was?" He was close to 60 when he retired, though his mother estimated his age to be actually 63.

Just as active professionals have a responsibility to their predecessors, so professionals about to retire have an obligation to their successors. I have often asked my older colleagues these questions:

- How did you treat those who might follow you?
- Did you give them opportunities to learn? To do? To make decisions? To make mistakes?
- Did you help them obtain greater understanding of their work and of the community?
- Did you include them in meetings with influential people or did you retain those contacts only for yourself?
- Were you more concerned with your own success than with the well-being of the community?

Some of us delegated junk and trivia and then prided ourselves on how well we delegated. Instead we should pride ourselves on how well we managed to pass on things of substance even if that meant assuming responsibility for some of the junk ourselves.

Until very recent years, in institutions for professionals we deployed academicians. I've asked myself, can we not think or write or transmit ideas to each other? Are we devoid of intellectuality? Of ideas of lasting worth? It is as though there is a dearth of elder statesman, among laymen and professionals. It is as though we have a system in which a person works and serves, gets old and gets out, and leaves little behind to think about. It is as though we are only pragmatists, incapable of creative thought. But without the transmittal of ideas, each new generation does a good deal of reinventing of the wheel as though we are unaware of Santayana's admonition about preserving and knowing history in order to avoid repeating the errors of the past. But there are elder statesmen among laymen and professionals, men and women to whom we defer, look to for wisdom, people who have been transmitting knowledge on which we built from generation to generation. Marcel Proust wrote, "The past is not fugitive, it remains present."

Stuart Eisenstadt, the former Assistant for Domestic Affairs to President Jimmy Carter, complained in a recent series of articles in the New York Times about avoidable errors made by people in high office, including the president of the United States, because of their ignorance of past experience. He issued a plea for the creation of a secretariat in the U.S. government composed only of career government employees of the highest quality who would be responsible for sharing with each new president and his appointees the lessons of the past.

In our study we did find a few Jewish communities in which retired professionals were used wisely and usefully. There they served not only as federation committee members but also as chairs of professional divisions in campaigns, as teachers in leadership development programs, as major forces in creating community archives and histories, as trainers of students and professionals, and as consultants to executives. One national agency has made a practice of retention of leading staff members, even octogenarians and nonagenarians, in part-time professional assignments.

THE FUTURE

In the coming years, there will be more and more retirees in our midst. Many are deeply concerned with the Jewish community and want to continue to use their skills on its behalf. We should strive to create a climate in which continuation of activity is the norm and in which the able professional who no longer works for pay is a volunteer, qualifying for a high rung on the ladder of leadership because of his or her years of service, skills, and knowledge. Those who make the decisions about who is invited in must be influenced to invite in the retiree.

In building the future, both retired and active professionals need to learn important lessons in ethical conduct. For older professionals, never try to make the younger person look bad in order for yourself to look good. For younger people, do not denigrate that which you inherit so you may lay claim to extraordinary achievements. This may seem an obscure lesson for professional people to learn, for it should be part of the moral climate of the profession in which we work.

A lot is said these days about self-acceptance and the achievement of inner peace. To say that peace within requires that one accept things as they are is a dangerous kind of escapism. Historically, people who have found genuine inner peace have been those who continued to work and to be identified with a mission of an improved world. Turning our backs on the world will not bring inner peace.

We should not expect retired people to turn away from their communities when they see things that they can do and ways in which they can be helpful, particularly when they felt they were part of a cause and not just doing a job. After all, when you do what you are supposed to do, life becomes what it is supposed to be.

RETIREMENT: CONSTANCY WITH A CAUSE

Presented on receiving the Distinguished Retiree Award from the Association of Jewish Community Organization Professionals at the General Assembly of the Council of Jewish Federations in Seattle.

November 1996

To be held in good esteem by my own professional colleagues from around the country with whom I've shared a common cause is obviously pleasing. I have cared deeply about the Jewish community and Jewish people everywhere. I spent so much of my life with people who shared that concern, like my professional colleagues and volunteer leaders in Milwaukee and throughout the country and in Israel with whom I have had the good fortune to be able to work.

My warm, good community gave me the opportunity 50 years ago—now almost to the day—when I was fresh from Army service to work within the Jewish community. The Holocaust had just taken place, and I knew then that I would be comfortable only if I was somehow helpful by working within the Jewish community. A few years later, I returned to Milwaukee as its executive, and years later still, in retirement, I was given the privilege of becoming a volunteer as well as a professional.

I have tried, like all of you, to give of myself. I believe each of us is enriched by what we give to others. I have received a feeling of worthwhileness with which I equate happiness.

Long ago, people of vision defined the work of professionals in this field not as a job, but as a cause. I have never understood how it could be possible for a retiree who had been involved in a cause to separate him- or herself from it. If I had in retirement walked away from the Jewish community, my conscience would have been troubled. There is a Jewish folk saying that states it well: "You can wash your hands, but not your conscience." The test of association with a cause is involvement. There is no statute of limitations on commitment to a cause.

At my age, one is nearer to the shadows than to the light. Retired people are frequently described as outliving their usefulness, and yet, how can a person live without being useful?

In the Jewish community we set aside the idea of of competition and teach cooperation and unity. We apply the words of the Psalmist—"Behold how good and how pleasant it is for brethren to dwell together in unity." And we give meaning to the words of Maimonides: "It is the duty of man to associate himself with the community."

Seasoned, experienced, committed professionals should be expected to continue with zeal to give of themselves. How could I, who has encouraged voluntary activity through all of my years, not grasp the opportunity to join with those who give freely of themselves to the community that I hold so dear. For me, idleness is the holiday of fools.

Indeed, there is something strange about retirement in our culture. People retire when they are so young. It is the pattern of our culture that a person trains for a job, hopes for a promotion, seeks to become an executive, and then having achieved all that retires—frequently to nothingness.

Retirement at 65 is ridiculous. When I was 65, I felt that there was so much that I was just beginning to learn. I have worked to ensure that seasoned professionals behave as elders, using their experience, knowledge, and wisdom, as well as their labor, to be useful. After all, no person can control the length of his or her life, but every person has the power to give it depth.

I need only to remind you that Golda Meir became Prime Minister of Israel at the age of 71, that Pablo Picasso produced some of his most famous paintings when he was between the ages of 85 and 90, that Frank Lloyd Wright completed the New York Guggenheim Museum when he was 89, that Goethe wrote Faust when he was 84, and that Georgia O'Keefe did her best work when she was over 90.

The great baseball pitcher, Satchel Paige, because he was an African-American, was not permitted to pitch in the major leagues until he was up in years. When pressed to confess that he was old, he responded, "How old would you be if you did not know how old you was?"

When I was young, I did not have the patience for things that might have taken a long time. Now, I take on tasks that I shirked because they would take too long.

This award for retirees carries with it a message of encouragement to go on doing what we are supposed to do, for then life becomes what it is supposed to be. The mission in life is to achieve not only happiness but also worthwhileness. Therefore, I try to be worthwhile and thus cannot contradict ever the intent and meaning of this honor.

PART VII:

LOOKING BACK

PERSONAL REFLECTIONS ON A QUARTER-CENTURY OF SERVICE

Presented at the Annual Meeting of the Milwaukee Jewish Federation.
October 28, 1980

A person has no control over the length of life, but has the freedom to determine its width and depth. This community and this work have enriched my life.

I have always worked with people in need; one of my first jobs was as director of an agency working with children at risk. But the Holocaust, by making me more conscious of my identity as a Jew, propelled me to work within the Jewish community. After I returned from the Army in World War II, I began to work in Jewish communal service.

I stayed in Milwaukee almost my entire career. I think I might have done well had I gone elsewhere, but I envisioned being part of building a model Jewish community here in Milwaukee, one that would be an inspiration for others. Paraphrasing a business term, I did not want to be just an opener; I wanted to be a developer. Milwaukee's progress has impressed people in other communities and burnished my own image

Edmund Burke admonished over 200 years ago, "Nobody makes a greater mistake than he who did nothing because he could do only a little." However, in Milwaukee, we have not done just a little; we have done a lot. Those closest to a community often find it difficult to measure its true quality. But people involved nationally and internationally, who have a broad perspective, perceive Milwaukee to be one of the best communities anywhere.

There is a line in Eugene O'Neill's play, The Emperor Jones, in which

Jones says, "Ain'ta man's talkin big what makes him big." I have always been unhappy with the idea that you have to be in a big place to think big. A national community leader echoed my thoughts when he asked me, some years ago when I had thoughts of working for a larger community, "Do you need to be in a big-big city to feel like a big man?" That question made me sensitive to a possible arrogance of which I would not want to be guilty. Whatever critics or detractors may have said of me could never match my own self-criticism. I am my own most severe critic. I have never been unwilling to expose my own shortcomings, and I have found that, by doing so, I have elicited the help of others.

I have never needed to trumpet my accomplishments to feel appreciated. Some professionals seek a great deal of visibility; they need to have their names in the public eye and their photos in the newspapers. Such professionals could benefit from a good dose of genuine humility. It would be good if some executives would have a passion for anonymity. In the same vein, I've often noted that some who make the most grandiose pronouncements about acts of kindness are the least kind, whereas those who make no claim to kindness are the most kind.

DIGNITY VS. TRUMPETRY

Dignified professionals prefer to help others to do good things, in the process earning mitzvot and resultant good feelings. I determine my own effectiveness by the number and quality of leaders in this community—I would rather feel proud of them than to make myself look good. I recall a discussion about the role of the executive in which a highly respected leader said quite seriously that the role of the executive is to make the president look good. The elected president or board chairman is the official head and during his or her term should be the person most seen and heard from in public.

We the Jewish people have never been able to separate ourselves from the crises of our times. Anyone who thinks otherwise needs only to look upon our historical experience. We have lived in dispersed communities for 2,600 years since the Babylonian exile. The expansion of the Roman Empire took away the Jewish homeland, the Black Death of the Middle Ages turned us into scapegoats , and the Spanish and Portuguese Inquisition made us wanderers. Hitler and his followers almost destroyed us. We have been the subject and the victim of history's longest hatred. Through it all, we have also remained the oldest surviving witnesses to the rise and fall of nations. We have demonstrated that when a people is determined it can survive and go on to greatness.

We have lived in a world that was divided for so long into two parts—one that wanted to spit its Jews out and the other that would not let them in. Israel was reborn out of the agonizing fire of six million ghastly screams. The anguish of our past is seared into our minds and onto our souls. Out of that agony and despair should come a new determination to build our people.

We would need a special language to describe the phenomenon of anti-Semitism—the singling out of the people of Israel as something to be against. It is more than anti-Zionism. The atmosphere of a country is created and molded by the words and conduct of its chief officials. France now is reeling from the latest strike by right-wing terrorists who want to kill Jews. This follows wanton terrorism in Bologna, Munich, and also in Antwerp, where bombs killed a number of Jewish children on an excursion last summer. In 1967, shortly after the Six-Day War, President Charles De Gaulle inaugurated a pro-Arab and essentially anti-Israel policy that France has pursued ever since. De Gaulle's 1967 characterization of Jews as an "elite people, sure of itself and domineering" resounds now in light of the horror that has recently occurred—and with the 1975 United Nations resolution equating Zionism with racism. Is it possible to proclaim the justice of the PLO cause, to condemn Israel, without creating a climate that is not only anti-Israel, but endangers Jews everywhere?

Israel and all of us have learned a lesson, and that is that there are times when no one will help us, except ourselves. We must ask these questions: How deep is our love for the Jewish people? How much do we care about the survival of the Jewish people? When we have burdens cast upon us, will we carry them? We have recently assumed a new responsibility—PROJECT RENEWAL—to make amends for the years of neglect when we did too little for Israel, and so we have an additional responsibility. But is it a burden? The warrior, statesman, Pericles shouted to his Athenians 2,400 years ago when they weakened: "You should not covet to the glory unless you will endure the toil." I say that if burdens are thrust upon us, we will toil, and burdens will be converted into opportunities.

We are a unique people with a sense of mission. The Jewish people brought forth many revolutionary ideas—monotheism, brotherhood, and living together in unity with diversity. Members of our generation, who were witnesses to the horrors of Hitler, who looked upon the vestiges of death, who saw an Israel reborn and the end of wandering for hundreds of thousands of Jews, have had to learn how to dwell in unity. We join forces to reach out to our people in the Soviet Union, in Ethiopia, and in so many other lands.

We have built the idea of federation, the successor to the *Kehillah*, on the sophisticated concept that people as individuals and groups can work collectively for the common good. It is that sense of unity of purpose that made it possible for us to pick up the remnants of our people and to help them live again.

We answer the cries of our brothers together by emphasizing the concept of tzedekah. In contrast to charity, the concept of tzedekah means that each of us is responsible for each other. It is such concepts that give us strength, quickens the pace of Jewish life, and makes it possible for us to work on behalf of each other.

This idea of federation means not person against person, but rather person together with person. Yet some can see only the particular problem with which they are concerned, the one that occurs only within the grasp of their hands and the sight of their own eyes. If each works for a cause in competition with every other person, if we have competition rather than cooperation, then inevitably we will thwart each other, as well as the progress for which we are striving.

The federation addresses itself to the problems of the whole community—at one time. It is a vehicle that makes it possible for us to dare to think of the welfare of all human beings as a practical objective, thereby rediscovering the foundation of our humanity. People can more easily confront their loneliness, their fragmentation, and their isolation by working with other people. No person, no group, can survive as an island. The issue is the capacity of people and groups to function together, to live as a community—a voluntary community, based upon the thesis that unity is possible without creating uniformity.

How uninteresting life would be if everyone thought the same, and yet how difficult it would be if people who think differently would only emphasize their differences. In the federation, we create a social union that permits the free expression of differences—differences that do not interfere with the capacity of people to work together to achieve common objectives. Absolute unity within a community is not possible; no matter how hard we try, people will have differences. The thrust of a community must be to have differences expressed, but to submerge them so we can move forward around those issues about which there is agreement.

Inflexibility was never our hallmark. There are all kinds of people among us; hence, we accept the idea that there can be all kinds of views. The extent to which a people accommodates itself to differences is an index of its social wisdom.

How easy it is to fight each other. How much more maturity and courage it takes to make peace and to work together. The poet John Greenleaf Whittier wrote:

Dream not helm and harness—

The sign of valor true.

Peace hath higher tests of manhood

Than battle ever knew.

The federation idea has been designed to give meaning to our faith. Our Judaism calls upon us to make a heaven here on earth now, rather than just waiting for an afterlife. The federation, as well as the synagogue, is concerned with *Tikkun olam*, the perfection of society, as well as the salvation of the soul of people. Those who do not carry out acts of tzedekah, who separate themselves from the community, do not understand what the synagogue or federation stands for. If we pray for freedom for Soviet Jews, how can we not support the federation, which finances the efforts to obtain their freedom and helps the refugees when they are free? If we pray for "Next Year in Jerusalem," then how can we not work with the federation to see to it that there is a Jerusalem this year, and in all of the years to come?

The Jewish religion has always preferred the right act, rather than talking about it—good deeds, instead of pronouncements, are what counts. As in the words of Micah: "To act justly, and to love mercy, and to walk humbly with thy God," and in the words of Jeremiah: "Seek the welfare of the community in which you live and pray, for its welfare will be your peace."

In the past, we neglected Jewish survival. Being fearful of prejudice, we emphasized integration into the general American scheme. We worked to erase the special qualities that made us distinguishable from others; we assimilated. We concentrated on acceptance by others, instead of acceptance of ourselves. There is a delicate balance between being part of something else and being something separate, and we neglected that "being separate" component. In the future, the priority of American Jewry must be to reaffirm the Jewish spirit and Jewish distinctiveness. We need to learn to nourish the special values we represent.

We have made great progress as a people in America, climbing faster and farther than any other immigrant group. Our grandparents were among the poorest of all. In contrast to other immigrant groups, in which young men often emigrated alone, many Jews came to America with their entire families. Among Jews, the family constellation was primary, and it led to the community's continuity. Our economic progress made it possible for us to sustain our agencies and institutions. However, we have been taught that money is only as good as the good it can do, that a shroud has no pockets, and that there is no special honor in being known as the richest man in the graveyard. Philanthropy is basic to our religious beliefs, the most important concept in the Jewish philosophy of life—not charity, but tzedekah, our noblest tradition.

When religious Jews are asked to specify the three most important things in life, they reply as follows: a belief in God, prayer, and deeds of lovingkindness. The eternally good and true principle of tzedekah leads us to practice consideration and kindness for one another, which has helped preserve us as a people for these thousands of years. We have learned to understand the admonition in the Ethics of the Fathers: "Honor not a man for his possessions. Honor him for the right use he makes of them." Our campaign leaders and workers know that their task is right and holy.

ELECTION OF THE JEWS

Soon we are going to watch a momentous presidential debate between Jimmy Carter and Ronald Reagan.* This 1980 presidential campaign is being held during a time when the Jewish people commemorate our most unique election, for the Torah portion tells the story of Abraham and Isaac on Mt. Moriah, about 4,000 years ago.

That election described in the Torah is strikingly different from the one now in 1980. There were no conventions then to nominate candidates, no demonstrations, no long nominating and acceptance speeches. The entire process of winning the nomination was compressed into one sentence: "And it came to pass that God did prove Abraham, and said unto him, 'Abraham.'"

That was the nominating speech—the shortest on record. It consisted of one word—"Abraham." And the acceptance speech similarly consisted of only one word: Abraham said: "Hineni," ("Here I am.")

The Torah goes on to describe how Abraham won the election, proving his faith by his willingness to sacrifice his own son, even though the sacrifice proved unnecessary. God tells Abraham: "In thy seed shall all the families of the earth be blessed, because thou hast harkened unto my voice."

There are major differences between the election in which we are about to participate in America and the election of the Jews as the Chosen People. Our President will be elected for a term of four years. We Jews were elected 4,000 years ago and we are still in office. We are the Chosen People. We have no opposition party because no other people really wants the job. Despite Tevye's appeal, God is not choosing anybody else. We are destined to continue in office until the end of days.

Now we have to have a platform, and it has to be in keeping with our covenant. The unique characteristic of the Jewish covenant was that God required of the Jewish people not a sacrifice of animals or of human beings,

---

* Annual meeting coincided with a debate by Jimmy Carter and Ronald Reagan, candidates for the presidency of the United States in early November. A large assemblage had dinner, heard, and watched the debate on large television screens and the annual meeting was conducted.

but a sacrifice of the heart—not ritual alone, but righteousness. The Torah does not say, "In your ideals shall all the families of the earth be blessed." Ideals without people to implement them are meaningless. The greatest Jewish contribution to the world is not Jewish ideals alone, but what we do to implement them.

I have always seen the federation as the instrument that binds us all together as a united, strong people, enabling us to implement those ideals: not to forsake the aged, to care for the sick, to administer to the poor, to provide a haven for the homeless, to educate the young about their heritage, and thus to perpetuate all of the things in which we believe, through counseling and work and recreation and camping to make people better and happier.

Jews in Syria and in the Soviet Union and Jewish refugees on the move are all communal priorities. Remember how we felt in June of 1967 and in October of 1973? Remember how afraid we were? How we wondered what would become of us if Israel were destroyed? How would it be possible for Israel not to be our priority?.

If you ask me what is our most important priority today, then I would answer: the Jewish community itself; our unity of purpose, our considerateness each for the other. I would say to you that we are living through a time of a blazing rebirth of the Jewish spirit and of the concept within Judaism that people not only have a concern for others but also have the strength and the means with which to express it. With all due respect to any agency or institution, we must think of all needs simultaneously—to enhance life for the poor, the rich, and the sick, the young, the old, with no distinction. Community is based upon the idea of peoplehood. It is kneaded into the very marrow of our bones and into all of our hopes and all of our dreams.

There are times when I confess to myself that I thought Milwaukee would be farther along in implementing its ideals. I have always feared that the job might not be done. But though I am impatient, I have learned patience. This is a community that has moved forward.

It is difficult to predict the future. Fifty years ago, no one foresaw the decimation of much of European Jewry. One hundred years ago, no one could have known that in the United States there would arise the largest Jewish community in history and that there would now be a sovereign state of Israel. And yet I can say with confidence there will be a better and better American Jewish community, and the finest of all can be within Milwaukee. We need only one thing, and that is a gathering of all of the forces of good will to examine the gaps in our work and to fill them, to acknowledge where we are weak so we can become strong.

I believe that all things that deter our progress as a community can be shunted out of our way. I believe that we are living through an era in which people concerned with specific, narrow problems will grow and learn that theirs are not the only problems. I believe that this Jewish community will serve as a potent example of how a people with a common heritage and history can make common cause. Those who lead this community, guided by their love and compassion, will work not just for survival, but to achieve the deep meaning of life. We will plan together, save life together, and raise money together. After all, what value do material things have if they are not used to enrich life? Is it not better to live richly than to die rich? If all that I believe is a dream, let me dream; and dream with me, for no individual and no people ever reach great heights without reaching for dreams.

In 1901, Herzl wrote, "Today I am forty-one years old. The wind blows through the stubble. I must march now at the double. It is nearly six years since I began this movement, which has made me old and tired and poor." He died three years later at the age of 44.

I am older now than Herzl. My task is so much smaller, and so it has not made me old or tired, and I am not poor. Yet, I have not done enough. We have not yet done enough. There is so much to do. Our mission is plain. Our task is clear. It is to build a united community here at home and to work collectively with all Jewish people to go forth as one, to pursue the dreams of our fathers and forefathers, and to inspire our young so that they will realize them.

MEMORIES AND CONTINUED COMMITMENT

Presented at my retirement celebration.

July 22, 1984

I have always believed in doing the deed for the deed itself—and not for the honor—yet this event does me honor.

I attached myself to Milwaukee a long time ago. Toward the end of World War II, the U.S. Army stationed me here to work in an Army maximum security prison. Irving Brodsky, who in New York built and led the largest conglomeration of Jewish Community Centers and outdoor camps for the elderly as well as children in the world, came to that prison to work with me. We were soldiers. I got there first and had seniority. My title was chief of psychiatric social work in charge of social and emotional rehabilitation. We actually helped people in that horrible prison. Jeanne Brodsky, Irving's wife, worked during that time for the Jewish Family and Children's Service, and I believe she was the best therapist they ever had. We all fell in love with Milwaukee, the warmth of the Jewish community. It was warm here, even in the cold of winter.

I needed to work for the Jewish community in part out of a sense of guilt. My father would have had me become a rabbi, but that, in my youth, stirred up images of a dour lifestyle as a yeshiva student. In a Jewish big city neighborhood with tough guys on every block and alley, yeshiva boys were scorned. I saw myself as a humanist. I believed in one broad humanitarian banner under which all of humanity would march. The Nazis and the Holocaust changed all of that. Conscience drove me, and I needed a role then in binding my people back together again by working for the Jewish community.

More than twenty years ago, when I was on my way to South America to work primarily with the Brazilian Jewish community on paramount concerns to Jewish life—assimilation, Jewish education, Jewish survival, community building and strengthening, among them—I stopped in Miami to see my father. Like all parents needing to show off his children, he introduced me to his neighbors and he was able to tell them, "This is my son; he builds Jewish life." That was a form of one-upmanship, a form of expressed vanity like "My son the doctor."

Some people believe that the only way to be big is to be in a big place, but I have deplored that idea. Those who live in the largest places are not necessarily the biggest people. There are big minds in big places, and there are big minds in small communities. This community has produced more national and international leaders than any Jewish community in America in proportion to its size. That made it important and very big. I felt the best possible achievement would be to create the model community, the one whose achievements would rub off and from whom others would learn. I hope that together we have taken the right steps in that direction.

My wife Eva and I have just returned from what was a very long trip for us—to the meeting of the Jewish Agency in Israel and some travel in France, Italy, and Switzerland. We decided to be in Normandy on July 4th. I had witnessed Eva 's tears at Yad Vashem, and I was struck by the depth of her emotions at Williamsburg, Virginia where she thought of the struggle for America. Now at the bloody invasion sites, including Omaha Beach and the American Cemetery, we looked out upon 10,000 white crosses and hundreds of Mogen Davids; overcome by emotion, we wept.

Then we had some fun. We were in Pisa, Lucca, Sienna, Verona, Firenze, Monaco, Monte Carlo, Avignon, Avalon, Salieu, San Remo, Montreax. Barbizon, and Fontainebleau. We stayed in chateaus, met Frenchmen, Italians, and Spaniards with whom we became friendly, and we drank Calvados in their homes. From portal to portal I gained ten pounds. So much for retirement—I'm ready to go to work. As Elmer Winter would say, "I'm not retired. I'm refired."

That I can arrive at this state of life suggests that I am no longer young, but then what is old? When I was ten, 25 seemed old. When I was 30 I was told, "Life begins at 40." At 50, I spoke of the past as being prologue. Now I have the privilege of being eligible for Medicare.

Great thinkers have had a good deal to say about aging.

- Jonathan Swift wrote: "Every man desires to live long, but no man would be old."

- On his 85th birthday in 1955, Bernard Baruch said, "To me, old age is always 15 years older than I am."

- Oliver Wendell Holmes wrote a hundred years ago, "To be 70 years young is sometimes far more cheerful and hopeful than to be 40 years old."

- The great baseball pitcher, Satchel Paige, when pressed to declare his age responded, "How old would you be if you didn't know how old you was?"

Nobody grows old by living a number of years. People grow old only by deserting their ideals. Thus I feel that I, like many in this room who are older than I am, will not grow old. There may be wrinkles on our skin, but not on our souls. Age teaches patience. When I was young, I did not have the patience for things that might take a long time—now I find that I am readier to undertake the tasks that I shirked because they would take too long.

THE BEAUTY OF A GOOD COMMUNITY

It is difficult to create the words to describe the beauty of a good community. In Switzerland, we stayed in an old chateau. We looked out upon great mountains reflected in a lovely lake, with lake and mountain fusing into white clouds in the sky. A camera could photograph it; a painter could paint it. Eva and I talked about other beautiful things—about the idea of Jewish community—of men and women and groups working and living together. Eva commented. "They say from anything you can make a picture, but from some things you can't make a picture."

I feel the Milwaukee Jewish community makes for a beautiful picture, even though the camera cannot take it nor can the painter paint it.

A TIME FOR SELF-REFLECTION

An event like this is also a time for reflection, self-examination, and self-criticism. Achievements with which I have been identified have been balanced by some errors. I have a good deal to be proud of and a good deal to be modest about. I know that I sometimes erred. People should never be ashamed to admit they have been wrong, in other words, that they are wiser today than yesterday.

I have not won every argument. There are those who feel there is a winner and a loser in every transaction, yet I believe that the key to victory is often related to who is the best loser. If I seem overly guilty it is because I believe that a sense of guilt is essential to maintaining decency, even in the face of achievement, particularly when operating amidst the realities of a world that is so often morally compromising. Our capacity for guilt is the basis of morality. An awareness of the gap between one's projected ideals and achievements is the catalyst for greater accomplishment.

I have dealt with many people in positions of authority and have seen some, alas, who were buried by their positions and others who always found someone else to blame for their errors. That should remind us of the importance of being able to blame ourselves when we have erred. When fools do something wrong, they blame others. Seekers of wisdom who do wrong blame themselves.

I have often blamed myself for what has not yet been done. I know that no one achieves all he or she sets out to do, for if we did there would be nothing left for those who follow. The poet Robert Browning put it this way, "Ah, but a man's reach should exceed his grasp."

PROFESSIONAL DEVELOPMENT

Throughout my career, I have believed in the vital importance of having high-quality, committed professionals—who are respected and treated with dignity. I tried to teach professionals with whom I worked, to retain their dignity even when some would take it from them. I taught that no position can dignify a person, but a person can dignify the office. We teach in our work the following:

1. Study and knowledge are necessary.

2. Too often, those with the greatest knowledge contradict the knowledge of what is right by wrong action.

3. We emphasize Jewish education, but what we truly mean is Jewish study, knowledge, and discipline to be followed by right action.

4. We emphasize planning our work, planning services, and planning of the work of the community before we act. We teach that luck smiles on the prepared.

I have taught staff members to be truthful, to come clean, and to be open with voluntary leaders. I always believed that those who make too many compromises with the truth should not lead. I have tried to teach consideration for others, cooperation not competition.

This community has been blessed with as many high-quality volunteers as any community anywhere. I say that, having worked with Jewish communities in many American, European, and South American cities. Our people are national and international leaders of Jewish life.

Some professionals create visibility for themselves—my preference has always been to create visibility for our voluntary leaders. As a result, informed national and international community leaders respect our community. We have been attentive for many years to the need to develop well-informed, skillful people who are equipped to be able decision makers. In contrast, some executives are happy with figurehead presidents who are briefed by the professional just moments before the meetings at which they preside, leaving the executive in control. Presidents who worked with me knew I would not let that happen. I look to the future in which this federation will continue to produce an ongoing stream of real leaders for our own and the world Jewish community.

The supply of good professionals is dwindling. Burdens are placed on shoulders now at a younger and younger age. It is necessary for us to find more young people who are young of body but old of head. Cicero put it this way: "Give me a young man in whom there is something of the old and an old man with something of the young."

COOPERATION, NOT COMPETITION

In our community we set aside competition. Competition is good in the for-profit world of business, but in a community, only cooperation is good. A community is a place where people and groups are brought together, where they strive to diminish differences and to work in unity. The capacity to unite is essential. In the late 1940s, it helped us pick up the bones of our brothers. In 1948, it helped us see an Israel reborn. In 1967 and again in 1973, we saw Israel struggle for her life and when the still youthful nation had its life almost snuffed out, our unity helped us stand with her and bolster Israel. That unity has helped us combat prejudice, be a leading force in the development of the democratic fabric in our society, and serve as an example for humanity.

Working together has become a benchmark, producing an understanding that a community must be aware of the needs of the people in it, the work of the agencies that serve the community and people, and the vision to look ahead and anticipate future needs and opportunities. Thus in 1948, well-informed voluntary and professional communal leaders had the foresight to create the Central Planning Committee for Jewish Service, a body inclusive of all of the agencies of the community with the federation at its core. Any human need identified by any agency was submitted to the Central Planning Committee for consideration, thought, study, and possible implementation, all in partnership with agencies. Decisions to create a new service or to expand existing ones were implemented by the whole community and each agency in keeping with its functions. No major service was planned or created without necessary study and review; none came into being without research and mutual agreement by the federation/community. Thoughtful people understood that, if each agency itself simply initiated services without regard to other organizations, the community would become a chaotic place, with the idea of federation diminished. Close association and cooperation became the community's mark, and there were few instances in which any agency strayed from that path.

That communal mood produced respect and unity in fundraising. In 1957 after consultation with all relevant agencies and communal leaders, and with enthusiastic support, the federation's Committee on Unified and Coordinated Fundraising came into being. Regional, national, and international organizations were asked to inform the federation of any need for which they wished to raise funds and to gain permission for their own fundraising efforts. The federation studied the relevance of needs and the appropriateness of their fundraising. Approving any fundraising effort and their campaign goals, the committee maintained order. Planning, budgeting, and fundraising were all synthesized into one overall process.

If I seem to be a bit preachy and hortatory, I suppose I am, for central planning and orderly coordinated fundraising are basic to work of any self-respecting federation/community. When agencies create services of their own volition with the federation expected to be reactive rather than proactive and when agencies independently mount campaigns for funds, others are bound to follow, inevitably creating tense feelings and a weakened federation. Communities cannot afford such things. Thoughtful communal leaders, who in the last four decades understood the requirements for progress, have developed a healthy, highly respected community in Milwaukee, which others attempt to emulate. Time is a school in which we learn; I hope that those professionals and volunteers who will lead in the future will have learned these lessons and build on constructive things of the past.

Community is a very sophisticated concept, not easily understood. I've often been concerned with actions people take that I know are not in the community's interests. Some people assume the authority to make decisions themselves or with a small group of like-minded people; they assume that they know what is good for everyone. Whether they are unilaterally creating an agency or expanding one, without examining its true need or worth and sometimes duplicating a service already in existence, I have come down hard upon them. I confess that it is not always easy to forgive those who speak of being for the community yet behave in anti-community ways. Sir Francis Bacon wrote, "We read that we ought to forgive our enemies, but we do not read that we ought to forgive our friends." But time erodes such angers and at this moment I am left with none at all.

If I were a rich man, then like Sholem Aleichem's Tevye, I would do many things. I would travel even more, for I yearn to see things, in particular to visit with Jewish people wherever they are, to reach out and connect with them. In the process, I hope to be of use to them, for I need to do that to feel worthwhile. Worthwhileness is in my mind equated with happiness.

If I were a rich man I would give much money to the Jewish community, the more the better. I would donate funds for training and developing volunteers and professionals upon whom the Jewish enterprise depends. I would help people know Israel the land, as well as Israel the people. I would establish educational programs, not just one-shot lectures, but educational programs with real continuity. And I would try to be a good model like leaders in this Jewish community are. I would reach out to others, in an anonymous way, using my means.

But in truth, I am a rich man—for although I have given of myself, as I have encouraged others to do, so have I received as all of you do. For we all are enriched by what we give of ourselves. I expect now to give of myself all the more, so that I can be worthy of the example of the people in this room—and the people who build Jewish life everywhere.

The Way It Was
Remembrances

While preparing this book for publication, some of my colleagues urged me to include some stories from my long career. I recall here a few amusing and interesting anecdotes of people of blessed memory, whose lives enriched the lives of all who knew them.

Irving Rhodes and his partner created the *Wisconsin Jewish Chronicle*, and its publication was the source of Rhodes' modest income. Yet he was chairman of the first big community campaigns: in 1946, at the time of sadness and mourning over the Shoah and again in 1948, a time of stress and then exaltation over the birth of the state of Israel.

Rhodes represented Milwaukee in the first national overseas mission in 1948. Nearly all the mission participants were people of wealth; some were movers and shakers, and others were part of distinguished families that placed them into a kind of nobility of American Jewry. These lions of American Jewry decided they needed a spokesman for their meetings with David Ben-Gurion, Moshe Sharett, Golda Meir, and others who were struggling for the rebirth of Israel. They selected Irving Rhodes because they saw in him an eloquent spokesman.

A few years later, in 1955, I began as the federation executive in Milwaukee. The campaign was not going well, and I made an appointment to discuss the situation with Irving one Sunday morning at 8:00 A.M.

I brought along pledge cards of people who had not yet made their gifts.

After reviewing these prospective donors, Irving said, "Let's go."

"Where?" I asked, and he responded, "To see these people."

I raised the question, "Now, so early on a Sunday morning on a dark winter day?"

Irving's response was, "What better time? We'll catch them home."

At 8:20 A.M. we rang the bell of the first prospective donor in Fox Point. Anticipating the arrival of her husband sent to the deli for the Sunday morning lox and bagels, the lady of the house eagerly threw open the door. She was stark naked. She shrieked and ran for cover. Irving blithely entered the living room and commented, "A parschein" (what a beauty). When the host arrived home, his wife, embarrassed, told him what had happened. He couldn't have cared less. He made a very generous gift.

Benjamin Saltzstein—Distinguished Attorney, Seasoned Leader, and the Source of Sage Advice

I was at my first Executive Committee meeting, and though I had met most members, I had not met them all.

There was some mumbling and staged whispers that I could not but over-hear, saying, "He's so young."

Ben Saltzstein, hearing those whispers, stated loudly, "Don't worry we'll age him."

A year later, I went to his house to discuss the campaign—it was dragging and we needed to strategize an approach to some potential givers.

Saltzstein commiserated with me when I pointed to the low quality of gifts from people deemed to be of wealth. He counseled me, "My boy take the money from bastards. If we don't, think of how little money we'll raise."

Samuel Sampson

It was decided, in the late 1950s that it would be useful if a few respected leaders of the community would go to Israel, learn of conditions and report back. Three community leaders and their spouses became the Milwaukee delegation. After they left, community leaders thought it would be proper and helpful to have a large community event after their return at which they would make their report. There would be a few speakers, Sam Sampson among them.

Sampson feared the event. He had arrived in Milwaukee as an immigrant years earlier and, with the use of his substantial wisdom, had become a very successful businessman. However, he never learned to speak English well.

Sampson feared that he might not be understood and that he would detract from the event. We therefore hit on a plan. He would dictate a speech to me in Yiddish, and I would translate it into English. We then reviewed the speech and changed words and phrases with which he was uncomfortable.

On the night of the event, a large dinner with an audience eager to hear about Israel, Sam gave one of the most magnificent speeches I ever heard.

It was all his—right from the heart. He brought the house down. There was thundering applause.

B.E. Nickoll—The Passenger in My Car

The federation office was downtown. Lunch meetings were generally held at the Jewish Community Center at 1400 North Prospect Ave. I would frequently be Ben's chauffeur to spare him the need to get his car out of the parking lot. He was a bit uncomfortable in my small car and would say, "Melvin, in this car I'm not proud to drive."

At one Executive Committee meeting, Ben entered the room and openly complained of riding in my car. The decision makers who were present discussed the situation. That's how I got a car. The executive was thereafter provided with a car with one stipulation: it was to be large and comfortable enough for Ben Nickoll.

Mishulachim

Visitors to communities—mishulachim—seeking donations for religious institutions in New York and Israel were commonplace years ago. There are fewer now and generally they only visit people in the Orthodox community.

One day a mishulach came to Ben Nickoll's office. His secretary in accordance with standing procedure gave the mishulach a generous check. The mishulach thanked the secretary for the check but asked to see Mr. Nickoll. The secretary pointed out that he already had the check, but he pressed and was ushered into Ben Nickoll's office.

The mishulach then asked Ben whether he knew the number of years that he had come to see him. Ben estimated that it was about fifteen years. The mishulach then asked, "Mr. Nickoll, if you had someone working for you for fifteen years, don't you think he'd be entitled to a raise?" He got a raise.

The mishulach got his raise and Ben Nickoll was rewarded with a more enthusiastic blessing then ever before.

Isaac Stern—Renowned Violinist, Friend of Israel, and a Wonderful Friend of Milwaukee

Milwaukee was part of the Large City Budgeting Conference in which community representatives met with leaders of national and international Jewish organizations to discuss their budget allocations. Among those organizations was the American-Israel Cultural Foundation (AICF) of which Isaac Stern was the president.

After one meeting, I received a telephone call asking whether I would be willing to meet later with Isaac Stern, his wife, and other leaders of AICF at the wonderful new building they had just moved into. I agreed.

I was impressed with the building. We brainstormed and strategized about the development of AICF. Out of this meeting grew friendship.

Whenever Stern came to Milwaukee to concertize he would telephone and I would visit with him. When he learned I was ill, he telephoned.

In 1962, at the federation's annual meeting, the speaker was to be Philip Bernstein, then the executive director of the Council of Jewish Federations. We were confident of his message, but concerned lest he would not attract the large audience that we were accustomed to having.

I telephoned Isaac Stern and I told him of our dilemma, saying that we needed an attraction, possibly a musician, and asking whether he could recommend someone to play at the annual meeting.

Isaac thought for a moment and he said, "Mel, I've got somebody for you. I'll send him. Don't worry—he'll be good—you're going to like it."

The event was moved from the auditorium to the gymnasium of the Jewish Community Center, for now we expected a large crowd. We had to cover the gym floor and build a temporary stage.

The evening of the event came. The speaker spoke, and he was good. And now our special guest was announced. A boy climbed up the stairs to the makeshift stage, put a violin under his chin, and began to play: it was Yitzhak Perlman, then fifteen years old. The audience was entranced. To our knowledge, it was the first time that he had performed in the United States outside of New York City—this in a gymnasium. He was accompanied by his mother.

His performance fee was $250.00 and transportation costs. When I would see Perlman later when he was so highly paid, he would remind me of how much we had paid him and I would remind him that the deal was $250.00 and all the candy he could eat—and that he had eaten plenty of it.

B.J. Samson and Jewish Education

As the new president of the federation in 1958, B.J. agreed to make the rounds of agencies to get to understand them.

We ended the day-long tour at the East Side Hebrew School. B.J. found it interesting, but then he recognized children of families he knew, families that were well off economically.

B. J. raised a question. He asked whether we were subsidizing the cost of education for these children, pointing out that their parents could easily pay the full cost or more.

I then asked him, what would we do if the parents were not interested enough to pay suitably?

And he responded, "Then the children could not have the service."

I agreed that paying for religious school was a parental responsibility. However, if they were not willing to pay, their children would not gain Jewish knowledge or learn about Jewish life. The parents might not consider that a great loss. But the federation would, because we were eager to perpetuate the community and Jewish survival. Our interest in the Jewish education then could be greater than that of the parents.

From that point on, B.J. became an advocate of good Jewish education paid for by the community to the extent possible.

Labor Zionists—The Guide for Giving

It was in the late 1950s. In those days, the campaign cabinet decided with substantial chutzpah to publish a guide for giving.

The guide was created and went to every family. It listed on one side brackets of income, and on the other side it recommended gifts related to each category of income.

I went to the office on that Monday steeled for angry telephone calls.

People would shout and scream. They would be asking, who are we to tell anybody how to give? They'd be offended—they would accuse us of being overly aggressive and demanding.

On Monday morning as I waited, the telephone calls did come. The first was from Arthur Spiegel, a Labor Zionist leader dedicated to Israel.

Arthur shouted, "What did you do to us?"

I said quietly that I hope no one was offended.

Arthur reacted, "What are you talking about? Our people give more than your suggested amounts. You're asking for too little. You're going to wreck the campaign. You're going to hurt Israel."

The next call was from Morris Weingrod, who suggested that we confess publicly that somehow we've made an error and that we send out a new table suggesting more money. He too was a product and leader of the Labor Zionist movement.

What a shining example of a group's commitment to its vision.

Martin Stein—Solicitor

When Marty solicited for a cause in which he believed, he did it seriously. He felt most people never gave to the maximum degree possible.

It was late 1984. Marty had been the campaign chairman a few years earlier. Now he was to be the incoming president of the federation. Marty telephoned me to say that he wanted to solicit me for the campaign. I replied that he could use his time with greater profit by soliciting others, but he insisted on meeting me.

Marty came to my office and said that he had volunteered to solicit me. I told him my economic situation had changed. I had been for the two years prior the largest giver of all professionals nationally, with the exception of the executive of the United Jewish Appeal. But I was now retired.

Marty listened to me sympathetically and now I began to cringe, feeling my arm was about to be twisted. When Marty opened his mouth, he protested. He did twist my arm—to give less. We bargained, with me pressing to give more and he pressing me to give less. We finally arrived at an amicable settlement.

Stockholm, Sweden—May 1975

It was a meeting of the European Council of Jewish Communities, for which I served as consultant. The office was in Paris but this meeting was held in Stockholm to celebrate the 200th anniversary of the founding of the Jewish community of Sweden.

I was invited to dinner with Fritz Hollander, originally German but now a Swedish citizen and president of the European Council of Jewish Communities; he was a businessman of international importance. At dinner were two people from a Jewish community in an Eastern European communist country thoroughly controlled by the Soviet Union and one other guest.

The two Jewish people from the communist country were asking for a substantial amount of money to build a Jewish community center. As they discussed the matter with Hollander, I suggested that the Council approve the idea when I felt a sharp kick in my leg. I realized it was best to keep my mouth shut. At the conclusion of the discussion in which a promise was made to attempt to be helpful, the matter was explained to me. The representatives of this communist country were ordered by their government officials to get money because the country was short of hard currency. The painful lesson I learned was that in diplomacy it is sometimes necessary to talk and not to act. When the Soviet Union fell along with its surrounding allies, the community got money from the American Jewish Joint Distribution Committee for a wonderful new community center.

Yitzhak Rabin—1968

Yitzhak Rabin, Chief of Staff of the Israel Defense forces during the 1967 Six-Day War, was the Ambassador of Israel to the United States the next year. He had come to Milwaukee to speak at a federation event.

Rabin was greeted at the airport, and he and his entourage drove to the Pfister Hotel. The Milwaukee police provided a substantial escort—a police car in front and two in back.

We arrived at the Pfister Hotel and went up to the suite, with the police following. At the suite, four detectives positioned themselves, two on each side of the door, for security purposes. We walked into the room, and Rabin removed his jacket. After doing so, he removed a pistol. I turned to him and asked, "Have you been carrying that with you all of this time?"

Rabin responded, "Do you think I'd count on them?" pointing to the police stationed outside his door.

Milwaukee's Wonderful Women

In the 1950s the campaign was not going well, people were discouraged, and the mood was down. The women leaders were concerned. They took counsel with each other and with me.

At a strategy session, I met with Esther Cohen, Ann Agulnick, Margaret Miller, Charlotte Bernhard, and Evelyn Lazarus. They thought that the spirit of the campaign could be lifted by having the women make their gifts first, which would have a positive impact on their spouses' gifts.

So at that year's major Women's Division event, the women made their pledges in the afternoon and for the first time their spouses joined them at a dinner, where both a federation leader and Richard Tucker, the famed Metropolitan opera star, spoke. As the meeting went on, spirits were high, and there was a sense of drama in the room. The speakers who had come to inspire were themselves inspired. They turned to the women, and one of them, feeling overwhelmed, asked, "What's going on in this room?"

The indomitable Esther Cohen responded, "Do you how much love there is this room?"

The strategy of the women to lift the campaign was never shared. They had inspired men, including their own husbands, to give more money than they had intended.

Up until the 1960s there was felt to be no need for a year-round director of the Women's Division. The work was encompassed within the duties of other federation staff members.

In the mid-1960's Mary Waisman was asked to chair the Women's Division campaign. She had done it in two previous years, but now felt there was a need for a staff person to work exclusively with the women. However, we were not ready then to employ a full-time professional so we decided on a plan: we would ask Ann Agulnick if she would be willing to take on the chore.

I called Ann, who was visiting her children in Indianapolis, and told her that she had a job. She asked for an explanation. I told her she was now the director of the Women's Division for the campaign. I could hear Ann's chuckle and her quick response, "Okay."

Ann fit right in. She was a wonder to have. The first directors of the Women's Division were volunteers, though we insisted on some form of salary, for after all, were they not doing professional jobs? By and large they accepted the money and then turned it back in the form of special gifts.

Women showed the way. Ours was a wonderful and absolutely inspirational Women's Division.

Paris 1970

I was in Paris in 1970 working alongside European Jewish leaders on the restructuring of the Jewish Agency for Israel. At an opening meeting, the handful of Americans invited were dispersed among the Europeans at various tables.

On my right sat the leader of Spanish Jewry, Max Mazin; on my left the leader of Finnish Jewry from Turko. Only one of us could speak Finnish, only one Spanish, only one—me—English.

We communicated with each other and somehow learned that we were each born in the same area of Eastern Poland near Bialystok. I was brought out from there as an infant, and the other two left when they were adults. We discovered we had one common language—Mamaloshen—Yiddish—and we enjoyed our conversation in our first language.

Jews live all over the world. Though dispersed we are all on the same journey.